WORKING WITH OUR 4-D STUDENTS

(Defiant, Difficult, Disrespectful & Disruptive)

"Education Needs a Champion"

by

LARRY D. DAVIS

DEDICATION

I dedicate this book to all the people that have prayed with me and offered prayer for me. As I started to put the materials together for this book, a friend of mine from Boston, Massachusetts called me just to say hello. It is important that I share with you that I had not spoken with this friend in several months and I have never discussed my work with anyone until it is complete. After we said our hello's, she informed me that she had a prophesy that she needed to share with me.

"Larry, God showed me a vision of a book that you are working on. The book has information that you have collected from educators from across the U.S. while you were presenting at educational conferences. In my vision, God showed me your book would be a bestseller. Larry, I know that you do not believe me, so tell me – are you working on 2 books right now? You need to finish the book that you have been putting off for three years first. Then you should finish the book that I saw in my vision."

I believe you; I have not spoken with you in months – how would you know that I was working on a book, not to mention two books? She went on to tell me that I would get former NFL referee Jim Tunney to write the foreword for my book. If you turn the page, you will see that Dr. Jim Tunney, former NFL referee did write the foreword to this book.

Imago Dei, "the image of God"

ACKNOWLEDGEMENT

I would like to acknowledge my brothers and sisters. I grow up in a household with seven siblings, two older brothers, four older sisters and a younger sister. A household filled with the most memorable moments and holiday celebrations. I am number seven of eight. Because I was the seventh child of eight, I was able to look, listen, and learn from each of them. I want to take this time to acknowledge each of my brothers and sisters by name and in order: Gloria Castle oldest sister, Everett Angle oldest brother (rest in love 2009), James Davis third oldest, Yolanda Kindles fourth oldest (rest in love 2018), Magnolia Howard fifth oldest, Beatrice Davis sixth oldest and Johnetta Edwards the youngest sibling. I would also like to acknowledge my last living aunt Elois Johnson. I love each of you, I would like to share James 5:16 Therefore confess your sins to each other and pray for each other so that you may be healed. The prayer of a righteous person is powerful and effective.

Table of contents

FOREWORD

by Dr. Jim Tunney

The first thing that caught my eye, and hopefully yours as well, is that Author Davis is writing about *his* students. All too often authors are telling you about what to do and how to handle your students without first-hand knowledge. Larry D. Davis is one who "walks-his-talk" having been there with 4-D students.

I have been there as well, having worked is schools, both junior high (aka middle) and senior high schools for over 30 years as a classroom teacher, counselor, after school athletic coach, registrar, assistant principal (which in my time was called vice-principal), high school principal, and district superintendent. Most of the schools in which I worked were called inner-city. My first school assignment was a 6-year (junior-senior [grades 7-12]) high school located in Lincoln Heights, California. It was mostly (85%) Hispanic with parents from Mexican decent. We had many classes in English As a Second Language (ESL) with most of those students being the first in their family to attend – and/or graduate -- from high school.

Author Davis lists many characteristics important to attain success with student with these disabilities. Disabilities is the correct description. Many teachers along with the public as well as parents often label these disruptive students as "dumb," "ignorant," and the like, but they are not necessarily so. It's the label attached that is dumb.

These so-called 4-D students just seem to not be able to be in-step with educational mores and thereby rebel with whatever type of "D" that best fits their needs. Author Davis along with this writer believes in the approach "every kid a winner." No one likes to fail in anything he or she does. Everyone wants to be successful. It's our task to find a way to make that happen.

To have a success with our students the author uses the acronym "BRACE" which, briefly, he describes as B= Beliefs; R=Relation-ships; A=Attitude; C=Culture; and E=Environment. The challenge is for you to explore these 5 approaches, which will give you a guideline for success.

When the author delves into the subject of corporal punishment, he strikes a familiar cord with this writer. I was fortunate to be raised in a loving family, but often with "old-school" philosophy. The use of the paddle by my school-teacher father was (all-too-often) a familiar method of correcting my aberrant behavior. My father was the executioner, but only to me as the oldest child. Never would that form of discipline used on my sisters or, in fact, I don't remember it being used on my younger (9 years my junior) brother. Times were changing.

While my father was a strict disciplinarian, he taught me many lessons, and not always through the paddle. Fortunately, the use of the paddle lessened as I rapidly learned my "lessons." I must admit I used the paddle on my two sons, never on my daughters. Both sons have reminded me on its effectiveness. They in turn have not used that method on my grandsons. Better not!

Further, when I began teaching (circa 1951), the use of the paddle was prominent in schools in which I taught. I used it both as a teacher and administrator, but within good reasoning, giving the students (all boys of course) choices of the type of discipline in correcting poor behavior. I continue to have contact with those students (even though it has been more than 60 years) who have explained to me how it helped them. When I became a high school principal in a much different school environment and with a much different student body, I discontinued that method as well as prohibited its use. In today's school climate, I would do likewise.

While I have never been in direct sales with customers, I liken teaching students who display one or all the 4-Ds described herein to that of a sales person dealing with a reluctant customer. The customer must believe that you as the sales person is there to *help* him or her. It's that way with students and Mr. Davis describes it with word *trust*. When students trust the teacher, learning has a better chance to take place. When trust is there, student behavior improves.

The credibility of the teacher is paramount to proper student behavior and successful learning. Teachers establish credibility through their honesty and forthrightness. Teachers' humbleness and ability to admit their wrong, when necessary, will go a long way in establishing credibility. Students want to learn from teachers who they believe are in their lives to help them learn. Adopting the mantra "every kid a winner" indicates to the student that the teacher is looking for the good in them.

This foreword has taken the approach that I have personally experienced what the author is saying. Mr. Davis has outlined practical approaches and ideas that will help you. However, plans and ideas are just that until they are implemented. Action by you is  necessary for them to be effective. You will benefit from reading this book. Get it today.

Jim Tunney, Ed.D.
Educator, author, speaker and former NFL Referee

PROLOGUE

According to some of the nation's top educational consultants and or most literature, the top three topics covered in today's education system are scaffolding, rigor, and complex and compelling text. In this time of high stakes accountability and attempts to close the achievement gap, it is easy to see why scaffolding, rigor, and complex and compelling text are at the forefront of most educational experts list. I don't disagree with any of the previous mentioned topics. However, I would add numeracy to this list. We cannot forget math and science. Let us talk about scaffolding, rigor, and complex and compelling text in greater detail.

Back in 1976, researchers David Wood, Gail Ross, and Jerome Bruner coined the term "scaffolding" in a report entitled, "The Role of Tutoring in Problem Solving."

In building terms, scaffolding refers to a platform that is temporarily set up to aid builders. It gives them elevation and support.

In education, the mental image and symbolism is similar to grasp. A teacher acts as an "activator" who helps a student master a new concept. They use "fading," or the process of gradually lowering their support level (or scaffolding), as a student gains hold of the new concept, process, or task.

The following are six scaffolding strategies by Rebecca Alber.

SHOW AND TELL

How many of us say that we learn best by seeing something rather than hearing about it? Modeling for students is a cornerstone of scaffolding. Have you ever interrupted someone with "Just show me!" while they were in the middle of explaining how to do something? At any opportunity, show, or demonstrate to students exactly what they are expected to do.

Try a fishbowl activity, where a small group in the center is circled by the rest of the class; the group in the middle, or fishbowl, engages in an activity, modeling how it's done for the larger group.

TAP INTO PRIOR KNOWLEDGE

Ask students to share their own experiences, hunches, and ideas about the content or concept of study and have them relate and connect these ideas to their own lives. Sometimes you may have to offer hints and suggestions, leading them to the connections a bit, but once they get there, they will grasp the content as their own.

Launching the learning in your classroom from student's prior knowledge using this as a framework for future lessons is not only a scaffolding technique—many would agree it is just plain good teaching.

GIVE TIME TO TALK

All learners need time to process new ideas and information. They also need time to verbally make sense of and articulate their learning with the community of learners who are engaged in the same experience and journey. Structured discussions really work best with children regardless of their level of maturation.

If you are not weaving in think-pair-share, turn-and-talk, triad teams, or some other structured talking time throughout the lesson, you should begin including this crucial strategy on a regular basis.

PRE-TEACH VOCABULARY

Pre-teaching vocabulary does not mean pulling a dozen words from the chapter and having kids look up definitions and write them out—we all know how that will go. Instead, introduce the words to kids in photos or in context with things they know and are interested in. Use analogies and metaphors to invite students to create a symbol or drawing for each word. Give time for small-group and whole-class discussion of the words. This is done before the dictionaries come out. And the dictionaries will be used only to compare with the definitions students have already discovered on their own.

With a dozen or so words front-loaded, students are ready to tackle that challenging text.

USE VISUAL AIDS

Graphic organizers, pictures, and charts can all serve as scaffolding tools. Graphic organizers are very specific in that they help kids visually represent their ideas, organize information, and grasp concepts such as sequencing and cause and effect.

PAUSE, ASK QUESTIONS, PAUSE, REVIEW

This is a wonderful way to check for understanding while students read a chunk of difficult text or learn a new concept or content. Here is how this strategy works: share a new idea from discussion or the reading, then pause (providing think time), and then ask a strategic question, pausing again.

Rigor is understood in the educational arena as instruction that challenges a student's ability to think. Before we instruct our teachers to teach with rigor, we need to ensure that we have trained and equipped our teachers with sound and proven strategies in instructional rigor.

Endang Sriwahyuni offers five instructional strategies for instructional rigor: direct instruction, individual study, indirect instruction, experiential learning, and collaborative learning.

Direct Instruction is the approach which is also called teacher centered. Here, the teacher is all resources for students in the class. Examples of this method include lecturing, didactic questioning, power point presentation, etc.

Individual study consist of the teacher giving instruction to students, then the students do it by individually, and the students, later consult again with the teacher. We can write it also as teacher – student- teacher- student. The examples of this method include giving assignments such as essays, reports, projects, journals, etc.

Indirect instruction is more meaningful when students can seek and discover the knowledge. This methods includes: debates, panels, brainstorming, group investigations, etc.

Experiential is kind of strategy that is applied by giving students the experience in what is being learned. The experience is created through teacher designated of activities.

Collaborative learning, where the students are in groups to discuss, share, explore questions, complete projects, and interact each other.

Imagine Learning discusses complex and compelling text in this manner: to engage students at all levels, it is not enough for reading text to simply be complex. Complex texts can be boring and dry, making it difficult for children to engage.

A compelling text, on the other hand, draws a student in and gets them excited and interested in what they are reading.

Teachers can incorporate all types of classroom activities to help students view texts as intriguing and interesting, including sharing dramatic photos or works of art, video clips, poignant primary source quotes, or even their own personal experiences.

According to an article by Lily Wong Fillmore, Professor Emerita at The University of California Berkeley, and Charles J. Fillmore, past Professor of Linguistics at UC Berkeley,

"There is only one way to acquire the language of literacy, and that is through literacy itself...Complex texts provide school-age learners reliable access to this language, and interacting with such texts allows them to discover how academic language works."

Hopkins describes how utilizing compelling text encourages students to "lean in" and grapple with reading selections that may be above their current reading level: "At Imagine Learning, we are identifying and incorporating more paired selections and 'text sets,' creating opportunities for multiple exposures to important vocabulary and big ideas. Students may be reading about contemporary issues like endangered species, important historic events, or ground-breaking ideas from cultures around the world; if we can create some magic around the topic and make it compelling, students will work harder and achieve higher."

Numeracy is the ability to use mathematics in everyday life. Numeracy involves skills that are not always taught in the classroom – the ability to use numbers and solve problems in real life. It means having the confidence and skill to use numbers and mathematical approaches in all aspects of life. Numeracy is as important as literacy. In fact, it is sometimes called 'mathematical literacy'.

Scaffolding, rigor, complex and compelling text, and numeracy are key essential elements needed to support our students and ensure student success and academic achievement. As schools and school districts focus more of their time, efforts, and money in these areas, they seem to be forgetting.one major area that we must address if we are going to meet the demands of high stakes accountability and close the achievement gap. Scaffolding, rigor, complex and compelling text, and numeracy cannot support our students when they are not in school. Across the US, many of our states are placing students in in school suspension, out of school suspension, sending students in large numbers to alternative schools and school expulsions. We fail to realize that students do not learn when they are not in school. School districts are disproportionately disciplining students each year; it is my contention that this has become our biggest obstacle to student learning and success.

As an education system we will never see a significant increase in student learning and success, and we will continue to increase achievement gaps if we do not find away to keep our students in schools. When we take a closer look at the discipline data across the US, we begin to see how this data impacts African American students, Hispanic students, and special education students who are disproportionately disciplined across the nation.

School districts are sparing no expense when it comes to professional development targeting scaffolding, rigor, complex, compelling text, and numeracy, yet totally disregarding the impact that their daily disciplinary practices have on their academic data. The argument of this book is simple: If we choose to make a few well thought out and often overlooked actions in our everyday school culture and daily practices, we will make both swift and dramatic improvements in our schools. Understanding how to work with all our students to keep them in our schools and engaged in our classrooms, we could effectively close and possibly eliminate the achievement gap in America.

This book contends that the path to great schools, increased student success, and closing the achievement gap is simple. It requires all adults to make a determined effort to change our current beliefs, relationships, attitudes, culture, and environments. If we, can embrace the reality of how our commitment in these five areas will do far more for our students success and changing their behaviors than any punitive action or consequence, we will be taking steps in the right direction.

We will demonstrate how the power in changing our beliefs, building relationships with students, letting go of old perceptions and embracing a new attitude, and finally establishing an ideal and consistently positive culture and environment will work to create a school system where every child will experience success.

"Every child deserves a champion: an adult who will never give up on them, who understands the power of connection and insists they become the best they can possibly be."

Rita Pierson, Educator

Don't Smile Until After Christmas!

This is one of the most repeated and most often given advice in the education profession. Don't smile until after Christmas, what a sad thought. First, our students deserve to see teachers, administrators, and staff smiling and enjoying that they get to work with our children. What a refreshing thought, "children love seeing people who enjoy being there for them!"

Secondly, it is a depressing thought that as adults, we are willing to sacrifice four months of our lives each year to scowl and frown at children. Only to return to school in January and smile for the very first time. This is thoroughly confusing for students and could give the impression of our teachers being just a tad bit bipolar. Well, maybe not to that extreme, but you see where I am going.

No one knows precisely where "don't smile until after Christmas" began but let us collectively decide to retire it today. As teachers, our time will be much better spent taking the time to show our students that we like what we do and that our students give us a reason to smile in August and in January. How about starting the year by learning our students and setting an inviting and engaging climate in our classrooms? Not, scowling at them from the moment they enter our classroom, making them feel like an intrusion and an interruption to our day.

As an educator, here are two lessons that I have learned, and they hold. The first lesson is this, if you are not a day person – please get another job! The last thing our students need to see first thing in the morning is a frumpy adult mad at the world because the sun came up, and they had to get out of the bed before noon. Here is a suggestion, "get a night job" because you are in the wrong profession. The second lesson that I have learned is this, if you greet a student with a scowl or frown, that student will return the favor. In most cases, the teacher will inevitably be quick to send the student to the office because they have an attitude problem! When, in fact, it is the teacher who is giving off an attitude. Is this truly the first impression that we wish to make? There is always work at the city or county jail, where scowling and frowning are encouraged.

Don't smile until after Christmas; better yet – don't become a teacher. Our children deserve to experience an education system where the people they encounter cannot wait to love, celebrate, and teach them. How about this, "don't smile until you become a teacher and don't stop smiling from that day forward!" Will it be easy? No! Will it be difficult? Yes! But you are a teacher, and you have chosen to make a difference in children's lives! So, wipe that scowl off your face, replace it with a smile, and prepare to make students' dreams come true. Why? Because you are a teacher.

Dealing with Vs. Working With

Working with Our 4-D Students
Defiant-Difficult-Disrespectful-Disruptive

I know that teachers, instructional aides, paraprofessionals, and administrators alike are all looking for sure-fire strategies that will work with our 4-D students. Still, every student and every situation will depend on its own unique set of circumstances. I would like to point out that we apply the same rules associated with differentiated instruction to differentiated disciplining.

The book's title is **"Working with Our 4-D Students,"** not "Dealing with Our 4-D Students." Let us ask ourselves what comes to mind when we use the phrase **"dealing with"**? The following lists are things that we deal with:

1. You are on your way to an important interview and realize that you have a flat. The flat tire is a situation that we must deal with.

2. A severe storm came through last night, and you woke up to a leaking ceiling. As you walked out the door, you notice that the storm also uprooted your neighbor's tree, and it is now blocking your driveway. The leaking ceiling is something that we deal with.

3. You invite your friends over to watch the big fight; you spend all day setting up and ordering food. By 7:00 pm, all your guests' have arrived, and all are having an extremely good time. You and all your friends start to count down to the fight, 10, 9, 8 – 3, 2, 1, and surprise; there is no fight. Having the pay per view not work is something that we must deal with.

When we must deal with a situation, it infers that this situation is an inconvenience. Thus step-one is to "stop" using the term 'dealing with" when it comes to our students. This book is titled "Working with Our 4-D Students". When we use the phrase "to work with," it tells us that we are progressing towards and/or achieving a goal. My purpose in writing this book is to accomplish several goals. These goals include student achievement through increased academic time in class.

Help support and grow teachers through targeted intervention strategies they can use in the classroom. Finally, help school districts reduce the number of students receiving office referrals, students placed in in-school suspensions, and the number of students sent to an alternative campus for disciplinary reasons.

Astonishingly, the first thought adults think of when we want things to get better is, "We Must Work Together." However, when it comes to supporting our 4-D students, we choose not to use the term "work with." In more cases than not, adults often ask, "what have we done about our 4-D students" in lieu of asking, "what can we do for our 4-D students." The first statement implies having someone, preferably an authority figure, to deal with the 4-D student in question. The second statement, "what can we do for our 4-D student," implies a group of adults coming together for the betterment of children.

What we are about to discuss is not a one sizes fits all solution. In this book, I will discuss how our daily practices in the following areas will have a greater and more positive impact on working with our defiant, difficult, disrespectful, and disruptive students.

- Beliefs
- Relationships
- Attitudes
- Culture & Climate
- Environment

The areas mentioned above will have a more positive impact on all our students. So, sit back, buckle up, and prepare to "B.R.A.C.E." yourself!

The B.R.A.C.E. Model for Student Connections

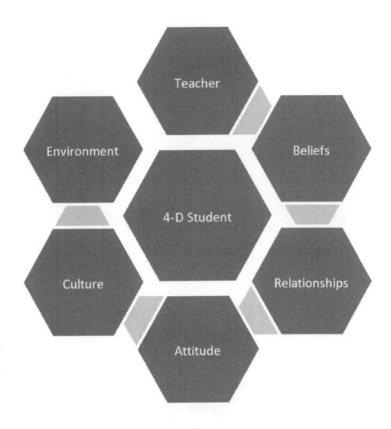

Beliefs = Projecting "Out" What Is "In" Us

Relationships = The "Desire" & "Actions" To Get to "Know" Our Students

Attitude = Humility, We See Our "Students" As More "Important" Than "Ourselves."

Culture = Our Daily Practices, Expectations, Standards & "Our Values & Philosophy" **Environment** = The Atmosphere & Climate That We Have Established

Introduction

THE SECRETARY OF EDUCATION
WASHINGTON, DC 20202

November 22, 2016

Dear Governors and Chief State School Officers:

As Governors and Chief State School Officers, you know that public schools are crucial places for nurturing all children's unique gifts and developing the knowledge and skills they need to grow and thrive in our democracy. I appreciate the work you are doing— from early learning to post-secondary education — to support our schools in this mission. To fulfill this mission of promoting the positive development of our youth, a school must first ensure that no harm occurs to the children and young people entrusted into its care. For this reason, I write to you to call your attention to practice in some schools — the use of corporal punishment — which is harmful, ineffective, and often disproportionately applied to students of color and students with disabilities, which states have the power to change.

If you have not already, I urge you to eliminate this practice from your schools instead of promoting supportive, effective disciplinary measures. Many of you, and your districts and educators, are leading the way in rethinking how to create positive school climates and improve discipline practices in your schools, and eliminating corporal punishment is a critical piece of that work. Corporal punishment can hinder creating a positive school climate by focusing on punitive measures to address student misbehavior rather than positive behavioral interventions and supports. Corporal discipline also teaches students that physical force is an acceptable means of solving problems, undermining efforts to promote nonviolent techniques for conflict resolution.

In-school corporal punishment generally entails school personnel intentionally inflicting pain on a child as a punishment or to change the child's behavior. As the accompanying map shows, today, 22 states allow the use of corporal punishment in their schools to punish students or to influence student behavior otherwise. Notably, the very acts of corporal punishment that are permissible when applied to children in schools under some state laws would be prohibited as criminal assault or battery when applied to adults in the community in those very same states. States should also be aware that in-school corporal punishment is often not applied equally to all students. Instead, the use of in-school corporal punishment tends to be associated with characteristics such as a child's race, national origin, sex, and/or disability status. Significantly, such disparities can raise concerns of unlawful race, national origin, sex, or disability discrimination under federal law, although statistics alone would not end an inquiry. According to the Department's Civil Rights Data Collection (CRDC), over 110,000 students, were subject to corporal punishment in school during the 2013-2014 academic year. Yet in-school corporal punishment and its related harm disproportionately impact students of color. Based on the 2013-2014 CRDC, approximately 40,000 — or more than one-third — of those students who were subjected to corporal punishment are black; black students, by comparison, make up only 16 percent of the total public-school student population. Similarly, in states where students were subjected to corporal punishment, black boys were 1.8 times as likely as white boys to be subject to corporal punishment. Black girls were 2.9 times as likely as white girls to be subject to corporal punishment. Disparities in the use of in-school corporal punishment are not limited to race, boys, and students with disabilities experience higher corporal punishment rates. Based on the 2013-2014 CRDC, boys represented about 80 percent of all students experiencing corporal punishment. Similarly, in nearly all the states where the practice is permitted, students with disabilities were subjected to corporal punishment at higher rates than students without disabilities. These data and disparities shock the conscience.

The use of corporal punishment is also ineffective as a strategy to address inappropriate behavior. When used to compel behavioral change, corporal punishment often has antithetical results; for example, physical punishment may make a child more aggressive, defiant, and oppositional.13

Moreover, it can be detrimental to a child's health and well-being and may have lifelong repercussions. Research shows, for example, that children who experience physical punishment are more likely to develop mental health issues, including alcohol and drug abuse or dependence, mood disorders, anxiety disorders, and other personality disorders. The excessive use of corporal punishment has been shown to be associated with antisocial behavior in children and later when they reach adulthood.

Beyond its alarming health implications, corporal punishment in school is also associated with negative academic outcomes. Research shows, for example, that corporal punishment can impact children's cognitive functioning, potentially affecting verbal capacity, brain development, and the ability to solve problems effectively. Studies also indicate that students as young as those in pre-school who experience corporal punishment tend to perform at lower levels than peers who have not been subjected to such practices on academic achievement and social competence measures.

While some may argue that corporal punishment is a tradition in some school communities, past practice alone cannot be enough rationalization for continuing to engage in actions that have been proven to have short- and long-term detrimental effects. Indeed, many practices were previously legal in the United States but which we would not tolerate today. There is a growing consensus that we simply cannot condone state-sanctioned violence against children in school.

A long list of education, medical, civil rights, disabilities, and child advocacy groups, including the National Education Association, American Federation of Teachers, American Psychological Association, American Academy of Pediatrics, and many others have also been calling for a ban on this practice and citing the harmful long-term effects on children, and the need to keep physical violence out of the educational environment. Corporal punishment has also been banned in Head Start Programs, Department of Defense-run schools, U.S. prisons and U.S. military training facilities, and most juvenile detention facilities. As the evidence against corporal punishment mounts, so does our moral responsibility to eliminate this practice.

A safe, supportive school environment is critical to support effective teaching and learning. I applaud the many states, districts, and educators leading the way in fostering positive school climates and improving discipline practices through proven strategies. The successful implementation of positive behavioral interventions and supports and better training and professional development for educators will equip them to administer supportive school discipline approaches in non-discriminatory and effective ways. Still, others are exploring promising avenues, such as the greater involvement of mental health specialists and the use of restorative justice practices.

I am glad to recognize and support these states and districts through our "Rethink Discipline" initiative. We can do more to support school discipline practices that foster safe, supportive, and productive learning environments. One critical step would be to cease the use of corporal punishment in all our public schools. It is difficult for a school to be considered safe or supportive if its students fear being physically punished by the adults who are charged with supporting their learning and their future.

11

School-sponsored corporal punishment is ineffective, but a harmful practice and disproportionally impacts students of color and students with disabilities. This practice has no place in the public schools of a modern nation that plays such an essential role in advancing and protecting civil and human rights. Thank you for your leadership in reconsidering this practice and ensuring that schools are safe and supportive places where all students can thrive.

Sincerely,

John B. King, Jr.

Corporal Punishment

Since the drafting of this letter, there are now 19 states that allow for corporal punishment. (please see the US map below)

STATES THAT HAVE LAWS PERMITTING CORPORAL PUNISHMENT IN SCHOOLS

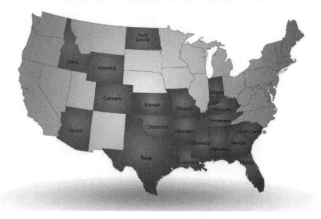

If I forgot to mention it, I am from the largely red state at the bottom of the map, "Texas." Here are the Texas Assault and Battery Laws and Animal Cruelty Laws:

Statute: Texas Penal Code § 22.01, et seq.
Statutory Definition of Assault

A person commits an offense if the person:

Intentionally, knowingly, or recklessly causes bodily injury to another, including the person's spouse.

Intentionally or knowingly threatens another with imminent bodily injury, including the person's spouse. Intentionally or knowingly causes physical contact with another when the person knows or should reasonably believe that the other will regard the contact as offensive or provocative.

Classification of the Offences

Class C misdemeanor: If a person threatens another with bodily harm or causes physical contact provocatively or offensively and no other aggravating factors are present.

Class B misdemeanor: This happens when a person commits an assault against a sports participant during a performance or in retaliation for a performance.

Class A misdemeanor: if a person causes bodily injury to another, and no other aggravating factors are present, or if a person causes physical contact provocatively or offensively against an elderly individual.

Texas Animal Cruelty Laws
Tex. Penal Code § 42.092.
and Tex. Penal Code §§ 21.09, 42.09, 42.091.

In Texas, two types of laws protect animals from cruelty: civil laws and criminal laws. The laws are similar but differ in the penalties they impose.

In a civil case, if a judge rules that a person or people have been cruel to animals, the judge may take away their animals and/or order them to pay restitution.

If prosecuted in a criminal case, a person may face penalties, including fines, jail, or both. Those under the age of 18 are also required to undergo counseling if convicted of animal cruelty.

Texas criminal laws only apply to domesticated animals, such as house pets and livestock defined as "domesticated living creature(s) or any wild living creature previously captured" and subject to a person's care and control. Civil laws' scope is broader and does not differentiate between domestic and wild animals; however, civil statutes adopt a much narrower definition of what constitutes cruelty. Therefore, people could engage in actions that are not prosecutable under Texas criminal laws, but they would be held liable for their civil law actions.

Section 42.09 "Cruelty to Livestock Animals" and 42.092 "Cruelty of Non-Livestock Animals" of the Texas Penal Code prohibits a person from intentionally, knowingly, or recklessly cruelly treating an animal.

Let me keep this in perspective, "Working with Our 4-D Students" is not a book on each state's various civil laws. So, I will not go into the laws and statutes of all 19 states. However, being from Texas, I felt that our laws were fair game. Each of these 19 states has laws that make it illegal for one adult to hit another adult. They have animal cruelty laws making it a crime to abuse your pet or any animal physically. They also have laws protecting children from abuse of all nature. In a twist of irony or a loss of judgment, they still authorize students' corporal punishment by adults in their schools.

Too often, we forget that discipline really means to teach, not to punish. A disciple is a student, not a recipient of behavioral consequences.

Dr. Dan Siegel
"The Whole-Brain Child"

Question:

What Do We Do?

If our students cannot read	We teach them to read
If our students cannot write	We teach them to write
If our students cannot do math	We teach them how to do math
If our students do not know how to behave	We "Punish Them"
	We must recognize this as a "Teachable Moment."

The Trust Factor

You want answers and not sterile theorizing, but the tactics which are most likely [no guarantees] to work will depend on appropriate strategies. There is no "one size fits all" solution. In Steven Covey's book The Speed of Trust, he talks about "The One Big Thing."

One thing is common to every individual, relationship, team, family, organization, nation, economy, and civilization throughout the world. If removed, one thing will destroy the most powerful government, the most successful business, the most thriving economy, the most influential leadership, the supreme friendship, the sturdiest character, the most profound love.

On the other hand, if developed and leveraged, that one thing has the potential to create unparalleled success and prosperity in every dimension of life. Still, it is the least understood, most neglected, and most underestimated possibility of our time.

That one thing is "Trust."

Mr. Covey goes on to say that trust is in crisis, and he gives the following examples.

- Employees New Motto: "Trust No One."
- Companies: Urged to Rebuild "Trust."
- Both Side Betray the Other's "Trust."
- 20 NYSE Traders Indicted.
- Ethics Must Be Strengthened to Rebuild People's "Trust."
- Relationships Fall Apart as "Trust" Dwindles.
- Fifty-one percent of employees have trust and confidence in senior management.
- Thirty-six percent of employees believe that their leaders act with honesty and integrity.
- Over 12 months, 76 percent of employees have observed illegal or unethical conduct on the job – conduct which, if exposed, would seriously violate the public "Trust." **Now, Who Do You "Trust"?**

The above data is about adults and their trust level of other adults. One can only imagine what the data looks like from children's eyes about their trust of adults. If the absence of trust can topple the most powerful governments, lack of trust in our classrooms will inevitably cause schools and school districts to fail. In a 2017 article written by Tim Walker, he writes the following:

The "Trust Gap" in Schools...
And How Teachers Can Help Close It
February 23, 2017
By: Tim Walker

If students of color do not believe that school officials treat them fairly, a "trust gap" emerges that could impact college enrollment, even if they receive good grades, according to a new study.

What causes the "trust gap"? Extreme disparities in discipline and low expectations from teachers. Many students, particularly Black and Hispanic youths, develop a growing mistrust for authority once they perceive and experience these biases, says David Yeager, assistant professor of psychology at the University of Texas at Austin and lead author of the new report, published in the journal Child Development.

"When students have lost trust, they are deprived of the benefits of engaging with an institution, such as positive relationships and access to resources and opportunities for advancement," explains Yeager.

In an eight-year study, Yeager and his colleagues conducted twice-yearly surveys with white and African American students in the northeast and white and Hispanic students in rural Colorado, tracking them from middle school through the end of high school. The survey measured students' trust level by their responses to statements such as; "I am treated fairly by my teachers and other adults at my school" and "If a black or a white student is alone in the hallway during class time, which one would a teacher ask for a hall pass?"

The researchers found that trust decreased for all students during seventh grade – a time when a student is most likely first to detect unjust policies – but the declines were much faster for Black and

Latino students. Furthermore, these students were more likely to be cited for behavior infractions the following year, even if they had never been in trouble before and received good grades. School records revealed that the racial disparity reported by many students did exist.

"Perceived bias and mistrust reinforce each other. And like a stone rolling down a hill that triggers an avalanche, the loss of trust could accumulate behavioral consequences over time" – David Yeager, the University of Texas at Austin

African American students who lost trust in seventh grade were also less likely to make it to a four-year college six years later.

"Perceived bias and mistrust reinforce each other," says Yeager. "And like a stone rolling down a hill that triggers an avalanche, the loss of trust could accumulate behavioral consequences over time. Seeing and expecting injustice and disrespect, negatively stereotyped ethnic minority adolescents may disengage, defy authorities, underperform, and act out."

Trust

The previous pages talked in-depth about trust, our perception of trust, and the impact that the lack of trust could have on our jobs, our governments, and our schools. I cannot emphasize enough the importance that trust plays in our everyday lives. For this book's sake, I am not going to ask that we, as educators, focus on trusting others. No, for our students' benefit, I am praying that we focus on building the capacity for trust within ourselves. This seems to be somewhat of a derivative statement, asking a person to trust themselves. Once we can genuinely trust ourselves, we begin to trust in our decision-making and trust in our ability to impact others positively.

Steven Covey's First Wave of Trust is "Self-Trust."

Cores of Credibility

- **Integrity: Are We Congruent**?
- In this book's context, are we in agreement or harmony with district goals, policy, and procedures? Specifically, those that apply to students' achievement, student success, and student discipline.
- What are our "**Beliefs**"?
- **Intent: What is Your Agenda?**
- Ask teachers what our agendas are?
- Do we have the desire to build "**Relationships**"?
- Educating all students vs. Educating the students we like
- Increasing the academic time of all our students' vs. decreasing the academic time of our 4-D students
- Building Relationships with all students' vs. Making sure we get rid of all those bad students.
- Campus and District Success vs. Personal Classroom Success.
- Understanding the needs of our Students vs. Students understanding the rules of our classroom.
- Was the campus built to educate children vs. the campus was made to employ adults?
- **Capabilities: Are We Relevant?**
- What is our "**Attitude**"?
- Does our current professional development support our meeting the needs of every student?

- As a campus are, we equipped to meet the needs of a changed demographic.
- When was the last time that we, as educators, worked to increase our literacy rate?
- What do we know about our incoming students and our current students?
- **Results: What's Our Track Record?**
- What does our campus "**Culture**" contribute to our current data?
- Does our campus "**Environment**" embody the mission and vision of the campus and
- district?
- What does our disciplinary history look like?

No one can increase our ability to trust; only we have that ability. Will working with our 4-D students be hard, will it be trying, and will it be a daily test of our resolve? Of course, it will, but we are educators, and this is what we do.

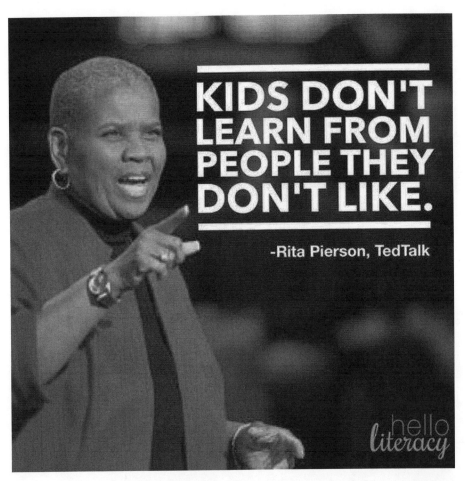

KIDS DON'T LEARN FROM PEOPLE THEY DON'T LIKE.

-Rita Pierson, TedTalk

hello literacy

"Kids don't like people that they don't trust!" By: Larry Davis

Meeting the needs of "ALL" your students starts with knowing who your students are.

Elena Aguilar

Beliefs

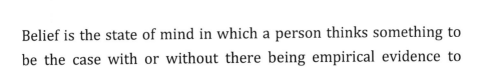

Belief is the state of mind in which a person thinks something to be the case with or without there being empirical evidence to prove that something is the case with factual certainty.

Below is a list of a few of my beliefs.

- When educators commit to student learning, our children learn.
- We must engage our students and build a relationship with our students and our parents.
- I believe in the work we do for children
- Supporting the efforts of my team
- Rising above expectations
- Supporting our strengths and pushing our weaknesses.
- Our campus must work as a Professional Learning Community.
- Our mindset must be "compulsory learning" for all our students, not just compulsory schooling. A person's belief is more likely to be personal, based on their experiences and culture, and are ingrained from their past experiences. I believe there is real power in our beliefs. Because our beliefs are a byproduct of many factors, as intelligent

people, as our knowledge grows and our experiences are enhanced, our beliefs can be changed.

"Please understand, this could include our religious beliefs; however, this is not what I am speaking about today." For this book, the author will be using the term beliefs to reference everything except religion.

I make a statement at every speaking engagement, during every presentation, and at every conference, I have ever attended. This statement is not meant to incite, provoke, or to anger the audience. However, I have never made this comment without having someone in attendance raise hand and challenge me on it! Here's the simple statement; "I became a much better teacher once I realized that my students didn't owe me anything. Once I realized that I owed my students everything that I had before me." Here is a simple statement of my belief; I never asked my audience to commit to my belief.

The following are lists of some responses I have had said to me in the past:

- As a teacher, my students owe it to me to pay attention.
- I have something that my students need. They owe it to me to at least try and learn.
- That is the problem most students have; they feel that we owe them everything.
- Teaching is not the easiest of jobs, so they do owe us at least that much respect.

- I do not get paid enough to deal with students who do not want to learn.
- Every year I am charged with increasing test scores, student achievement, and academic growth.

All the while, students are not held accountable for anything!

- Mr. Davis, I feel it is very disrespectful for you to stand before us today and say our students do not owe us anything.
- As teachers, we are overworked, underpaid, and highly under-appreciated.

These are just some of the statements that I heard and responded to over the years. I am pretty sure once you read the above comments, you may have had a few comments of your own. To me, that is the beauty in this statement; all the responses are based on their beliefs. And I have opened the door to bring them new knowledge, a new perspective, and create a paradigm shift in those beliefs. As I mentioned before, the real beauty, and we believe that they can be changed based on new knowledge and new experiences.

It is at this point that I am going to go into more detail. First, I restate what I said; "I became a much better teacher the moment I realized that my students did not owe me anything." Then I explained why I made such a bold statement. Educators, administrators, paraprofessionals, and central office staff would like for you to imagine a building field with adults and no students. The adults in the building have time to meet and plan;

they have time for the professional learning communities and have more than enough time to sit and enjoy lunch. They do not have to rush to the restroom between passing periods and try to make it back to the classroom in time. Having no students there during the day would allow the day to end at 3:05 pm. Tell me, what type of school do you imagine this would be? Here are the following responses that I received:

- You have a school that I would love to work at.
- You have the type of school where teachers never take off.
- You have a work environment where the quality of life has increased.
- You have a workplace where teacher retention is at an all-time high.
- You have a campus where teaching is appreciated.
- That would be the ideal school.

Now educators, administrators, paraprofessionals, and central office staff, imagine a school filled with students, a school with no adults, a school with no administration and no rules and regulations, and finally, a school where students are free to roam the halls. Tell me, what type of school do you imagine this to be? Here are some of the responses that I get:

- You have a building that I would not want to be in.
- You have an out of control environment.
- You have complete and utter chaos.
- You have the makings of a prison.
- You have a campus where learning does not exist.

- Sounds like a playground or recreation center to me.
- You would have the worst school in the state and possibly the country.

The final question for the audience of educators, paraprofessionals, administrators, and central office personnel is, "is there is anything else you would like to add?" I get the usual comments: we could go on and on about either scenario, but what is your point, Mr. Davis? Looking at the audience, I smile and say, "in the very first situation where we have a school building filled with adults and no children, what we honestly have is a building full of unemployed adults. In the second scenario, where we have a school building field with students and no adults, what we indeed have, is a building field with possibilities." You see, our students are the reason we have a job; our students are the reason schools exist, our students are another reason that funds were made available to purchase books, computers, desk, furniture, and all the things that fill our schools. Our students are the reason we wake up every morning eager to get to work and greet our children. Our students are the reason we seek out professional development to sharpen our saws and hone our craft. Our students are why we became educators, not the summers off and not all the paid vacation time that we get, but our students.

As the adults on campus, we get paid to come to work each day, plus we get holidays off, sick days with pay, and vacation days. Students are ordered to attend school by law, and if they miss a certain number of days, we report them to truancy. Does this sound like a "student-centered learning institution" to you?

Every school in this great nation was built to educate children and not to employ adults. When I look at all the things that have been made possible because I am an educator (an educator of children), I believe that my students don't owe me anything, but I owe them the world.

When I first became an administrator, I had a sign that hung over the outside of my door; it read, "the needs of children will always come before adults' wants." Yes, this was the source of many teacher lounge conversations, but every teacher in the building knew that we would make decisions based on our students' needs. For example, if the head of one of my departments came to me and wanted to rearrange their teachers, it had to be supported with student data. In other words, how would this change benefit our students? As an administrator, I did not approve teacher assignment changes because Mr. Reynolds had been teaching 9th-grade Algebra for ten years. He felt like he deserves to move to senior math because he spent enough time **dealing** with first-year students!

This last statement causes yet another stir! However, before things can get out of hand, I asked all my central office staff to raise their hands. The central office staff asked the following question. "What percent of the complaints that you handle throughout the year are the results of decisions made to benefit adults and not students?" Take a moment to think about it and not just blurt out the first number that comes to mind (I dismiss the central office staff into the hallway). Then take pieces of paper and pass them out to the other attendees, and I asked him to privately write down the percentage that they are expecting to hear. The attendees were given about five minutes to collaborate with others and share personal experiences. At the five-minute mark, I walked to the door and asked if the central office staff is ready to return? A member or two from the central office staff are brought up and share their responses privately. Now, I asked the rest of the audience to share their results with the central office staff. It never ceases to amaze me that teachers, paraprofessionals, and campus administrators will always predict the percentage below 30 percent. However, I am never surprised by their reaction when the central office staff presents a number that is 80 to 90 percent.

Eighty to 90 percent of the complaints that the central office deals with the daily result from decisions that were made based on the needs of adults and not the needs of children. I hope that once this information is shared with every educator in the audience, they will have a change of mind. The reality is they do not! The fact of the matter is about one-third of the attendees will start to blame policies, procedures, and/or the current administration. Not once do they stop considering that state board policy and local board policy could often result from decisions made based on adults' needs.

"You can't teach children to behave better by making them feel worse, when children feel better, they behave better." Pam Leo, Connection Parenting

Beliefs are the state of mind in which a person thinks something to be the case with or without there being empirical evidence to prove that something is the case with factual certainty.

Our beliefs are the results of our past, our experiences, our culture, and are often personal. The following is a conversation that I had at least once a year (if not more) with a colleague who did not seem to get their students. The following is not an original thought; educators such as Rita Pierson, Ann Lieberman, and Dr. Debbie Silver have echoed the same sentiment in their writing and teaching. Please take a moment to read the statement(s) on a conversation with another educator. Then on the page provided, explain if or if not, the quote has impacted your belief. Remember your findings, your results, and your final thoughts are yours and yours alone. So please be honest with yourself!

Students work hardest for teachers they like and respect.

When I'm asked, "How do I get the students to like and respect me?" My immediate response is,

"I like and respect them first."

Dr. Debbie Silver

Great teachers empathize with students, respect them, and believe that each one has something special that can be built upon.

Anne Lieberman

Do you believe either of these statements to be true? Why or why not?

In the space provided below, please give a detailed explanation of why you feel the quotes would or would not impact your current beliefs or the beliefs of someone you work with.

_____

_____

_____

_____

_____

What do you do as part of your daily practice, that embodies either of these quotes?

_____

_____

_____

_____

_____

Relationships

Dr. Larry Brendtro
Connect with Challenging Youth

Rather than wait for problems, one practices "preemptive connecting" with wary youth; this should be unobtrusive not to create impressions of favoritism. Connecting does not require a major investment of time; bonds can be built in natural moment-by-moment interaction. Small doses of connecting behavior are most effective. Forcing intimacy only frightens away youth who already are in an approach-avoidance conflict with adults. Those with histories of negative encounters with adults are strongly influenced by small cues of respect, humor, and good-will. The emotional brain signals, "This person is safe."

"Behavior is a form of communication providing clues about what is missing in a young person's life." John Seita, Reclaiming Children and Youth, 23:1

Webster's dictionaries definition of "relationships" is far too clinical of a definition for me. However, I do like this definition - how two or more people or organizations regard and behave toward each other. "the teacher-student relationship."

> Dr. Comer says, "No significant learning takes place without significate relationships."

Is it possible to look at the word relationships as a verb as opposed to a noun? A relationship is a noun, but so is the word love. However, being in love is a noun, but we express and show our love; love is most definitely a verb. How can we make relationships more action-oriented and move it from its current person, place, or thing and make it a living, ever-flowing act? We must focus on what it takes to build relationships and what it takes to sustain healthy relationships.

"The Gallup Organization's research confirms that the ability to develop relationships and a burning desire for success can be critical components of world-class sales performance."

Students are social beings. They enjoy being understood and accepted, feeling that they belong. Maybe that is why our friends, family, and reputations are so important to them.

Unfortunately, educators' value individual achievement over personal relationships. They excel at finding career success but are less than stellar at connecting with students' parents and other people.

As a result, their relationships often suffer.

As an educator, would you not love to rekindle that spark you once had with your students and be respected and understood by your peers? Admired for who you are by your superiors? Here is the good news you can! That is right; the way your students and peers perceive you and how your administrators view you is all within your reach, or should I say relationships.

There is a direct correlation between teacher success and student success. When students are successful, teachers get recognized; when teachers get recognized, promotions can happen. But nothing happens without first building relationships with our students. We all know what the data tells us. Students are more likely to come to school when their teachers know them, are connected to the school, and are engaged in their work. Known by their teachers implies that their teacher has taken the time to know the student's name.

As a teacher and later, as an administrator, I would be out in the hallways during passing periods talking to the students. Greeting each student and every class at the door makes our first interaction both positive and welcoming. My teaching experience includes eight years as a teacher and four years as a substitute. As a classroom teacher there was always a waiting list to get into my class.

The funny thing is, I assigned twice as much work than other teachers. In my classroom, the saying was, "leave all your drama at the door, and you can pick it up on your way out." This saying was for my students and me as well.

It was an unusually rough day, it was a Thursday, and it was the last period of the day. My tank was empty; no, it was well passed empty. I was not feeling well, plus during my conference, when I had planned on locking my door and taking a nap – my principal called my room and asked if I would take a class because the teacher had to leave. The teacher who had to leave was known to have the worst classes to compound it all. These students could be heard across three hallways. After going to that classroom and policing the students (not my finest hour by any means), I returned to my final period of the day. Still lingering from taking on an additional class, not to mention that class, my students walked into my class with me sitting at my desk. They were no louder than usual, and they came in and spoke to me (even though I did not greet them at the door). My class started with a very dry attitude: I checked attendance by calling out their names. During the process, one student said Mr. Davis; you know that we are here. Do you want us to say "here"? My response was, "student's if you don't answer, I will mark you absent." It was at this time, one of my freshman students' "Sarah" raised her hand. Looking in Sarah's direction, I continued calling the attendance. Sarah kept her hand raised. Finally, I acknowledged her and said, "what do you need, Sarah" in a very dry tone. By this time, the class had only been in session about eight minutes or so.

Sarah looked at me and said, "Mr. Davis, you told us that we were not allowed to bring our bad attitudes or drama into the classroom, that we had to leave it outside the door, and we could pick it up on our way out. You also said that this goes for you as well. Mr. Davis, would you please take your bad attitude and place

41

it outside the door?" You could have heard a pin drop on the carpet; it was uncomfortably quiet. I looked directly at Sarah, stood up from my desk, and proudly walked out the door, and dropped my lousy attitude outside the door. When I returned to the classroom, the first thing I did was apologize to my entire class and thanked Sarah for holding me accountable for following classroom expectations.

That day taught me a lesson that I will never forget. At that moment, I could have ruined the relationship I had worked hard to establish with the students, and why? Because I was having a bad day and decided to throw myself a pity party. When I got up and walked to the door and dropped off my lousy attitude, every student in my class gained a little more respect for me. By next morning news of Miss Sarah telling me to take my bad attitude and drop it off at the door had made it around the school. This school had about 2500 students and over 200 faculty and staff. The events made the morning announcements and later that month the school newspaper. Most teachers might have been embarrassed by all of this, but I spent the next few weeks signing students' newspapers and meeting the entire freshmen class. I remember my principal walking up to me and saying, "and teacher's wonder why you have the highest student success rate in the building," he laughed and walked off. Mr. Ric Canterbury, my principal, used to say to me that I was what he called a kid magnet. "If I could figure out a way to ensure every teacher that I hired was a kid magnet, I would be the best principal in the world." Mr. Canterbury, you were a pretty "dawg gone" great principal. Four months later, Mr. Canterbury promoted me to the administration. I became the first African American administrator in district history. He told me, "I didn't hire you for your color; I hired you for the kids." Mr. Canterbury was all about relationships; I learned a lot from him.

Before I leave this thought-on, Mr. Canterbury, Todd Whitaker says that there are two ways to improve our schools; (1) hire better teachers or (2) improve the ones that we have. It is amazing he does not mention anything about going out and finding better students.

A year later, I sat in my office as an assistant principal and the Assistant Superintendent, Dr. V.

Walks into my office, Mr. Davis, I just spoke with your principal, and I am placing you over all curriculums.

My goal for this campus is to become a "Recognized Campus" by state standards within two years. Mr. Davis, if this is too much to ask of you, please let me know? Of course, my response was, "Sir, this is not too much to ask." I forgot to tell you that Dr. V. stood about 6 feet 8 inches tall and had a very stately disposition. Intimidating, just a bit. Oh, by the way, I am 6 feet 5 inches tall, so to say that I looked up to Dr. V in more ways than one would not be an exaggeration. I asked Dr. V. a question before he left my office. "Dr. V., most of the teachers here, opened the school with me as their colleague; how do I evaluate them objectively?" His response was short and brief and needed no further explanation. "Mr. Davis, are the teachers helping or hurting students?" Then he turned and walked out of my office.

My teaching career has been about students and student growth; this was confirmation that education should be about the child and not the adult.

About six weeks into the school year, I noticed that I have a teacher writing an extremely high number of student office referrals. This same teacher had the highest failure rate in their department.

Not to mention, this was a core course that's state tested and monitored. For this example, I will call the teacher Mr. Williams.

Being in Mr. Williams' classroom several times a year, I looked at the data on the number of student office referrals and his high failure rate. I was alarmed. I made it a point to walk past Mr. Williams' room during my daily walks; I wanted to ensure that I passed his door during passing periods and not during class. I greeted Mr. Williams at his door, "how are you doing today, sir"? "I'm fine, Mr. Davis, how about yourself?" "I'm blessed, Mr. Williams because I know people like you. Mr. Williams, I know your conference period has passed, but if you could find some time tomorrow to stop by my office, I would love to speak with you. Please do not be alarmed; you have not done anything wrong; I would like to speak with you. Better yet, can we make it first thing in the morning before classes start?" "Yes, sir, I'll be there around 7:45 am. Is it okay with you?" "Yes, see you then."

The next morning when Mr. Williams arrived in my office, I met him in the hallway, and we walked in together. I needed Mr. Williams to see this as a collaborative endeavor and not as if he had been doing something wrong. I started my conversation on a very positive note, "Mr. Williams, you're one of the most popular new teachers on the campus. On a scale of 1 to 10, how would you rate your year"? Mr. Williams told me that he thought he was about four on a scale of 1 to 10. He said that he thought everything was going well but was unhappy with the high number of referrals he was writing and the lack of student success in his classroom. I asked Mr. Williams to tell me all the things he had tried this year to overcome these two things. "Mr. Davis, honestly, being a new teacher, I don't know where to turn or who to ask or what question to even ask for that matter."

"Mr. Williams, will it be okay if I shared some information with you"? "Sure." As a new teacher, one of the things I like to do is keep an eye on certain things to ensure your success. In looking at the data, there are a couple of things that jumped out at me; both are the same thing you just mentioned—the number of student referrals and your student success rate in your class. I have a question for you, how would you rate your relationship with your students? "Well, Mr. Davis, I know most of my students by name; I know which class they are in, but other than that, what else do I need to know about my students"? Mr. Williams, I am so glad you asked. Did you know there is a direct correlation between student success and how well the teacher knows them? "Please explain, Mr. Davis?"

Mr. Williams, you teach ninth grade. Did you know that ninth grade is often the last time a student will play sports? Did you know that ninth grade has the highest number of students

45

participating in school activities? My question to you, Mr. Williams, is this; when was the last time you attended a freshman football game, a choir concert, a freshman volleyball game, and/or a school play? "At the beginning of the year, the students used to invite me to events, but I didn't have time." Mr. Williams, do yourself a favor and attend these events this week. Make sure that you sit in the front row and make sure that your students see you there. If possible, at the end of the game, please acknowledge your students and their teammates. I noticed that in your classroom, you have an empty bulletin board. Take some time this weekend, if possible, to decorate that board as your school spirit board. If you are not good at this type of thing, ask your students to do it for you, they will be excited to do so. I will continue to stop by your room for the next three weeks and at the end of the third week, let us talk and see if things have gotten better. Mr. Williams agreed to attend several of the upcoming freshman events that week, and he will continue to do so for the next three weeks.

Over the next three weeks, I noticed a significant drop in office referrals from Mr. Williams' classroom. At the end of the three weeks, student progress reports went home, and at this time, Mr. Williams had one of the lowest failure rates in his department. Late one day, Mr. Williams came to my office excited, rejuvenated, and thrilled at his results. "Mr. Davis, Mr. Davis, I want to show you something. Have you seen my progress reports?" "I did what you asked; I attended several school functions for ninth-graders over the last three weeks; I also had some students decorate my school spirit board in my classroom and let them name the boards. After the first game, students started speaking to me in the hallway; as I attended more and more of my student's events, my students became more and more engaged in my class. I did not change the way I was teaching, nor did I reduce the rigor in their work, but my students seem to get it now. Mr. Davis, are you telling me that all I had to do was go to a few games' concerts and school events?

"No, Mr. Williams, I'm telling you that all you have to do for your students is to show that you are there first and foremost. When you started attending their games, their events, and celebrating them with your school spirit board, your class became about them. Before, your class was all about your teaching. Mr. Williams, our students need to know that they have teachers who are here for them, who care about them, and who celebrates them on this campus. Mr. Williams, successful teaching is all about relationships. The moment you attended the first game, you started building those relationships with your students." Mr. Williams went on to become the UIL Academic sponsor for math and number sense and continued to build positive relationships with students. Mr. Williams is now a kid's magnet!

When teachers know this, our students come to school and are connected and engaged in school activities and work. Student success equals a teacher's success, campus success as well as district success.

Here is one more thing that I did as an administrative consultant to a colleague of mine. My colleague was the superintendent in a school district with low performing schools. He was fortunate enough to be hired in March. Being a March hire gave him three months to observe his campuses, teachers, administrators, and campus cultures. In our first meeting, he showed me the district data. He informed me that he had done several campus walk-throughs with his administrative staff and central office administrators. The data collected from these instructional walks showed correlations between the data and each campus's low performance. Looking at the data, we both noticed is a high number of instances where substitutes were in the classroom when the regular teacher was out. We also noticed an increased number of student absentees, the average daily attendance for the campus in his district was around 85 percent. This result indicated that the daily average attendance showed that more than 15 percent of the students were missing school for some reason or another; he turned to me and stated that "he had never seen anything of this manner in teaching or administrative career."

Is there a way we can calculate the number of days that the teachers were absent each year? This was my question. We went to the PEIMS department and asked if they kept records of teacher attendance. It was not a surprise to either of us to see that teachers in the district were missing close to 12 academic days per year. In a district with 3,000 teachers missing 12 school days a year, it was easy to see that teacher's satisfaction, and morale was low. Three thousand teachers multiplied by 12 days; each is equal to 36,000 academic instructional days missed per year. There were two major problems; first, the students did not feel recognized by the teachers, they were not connected to the campus, and they could not be engaged because the teachers were not there. Thus, the students of the district did not feel safe nor recognize love. Secondly, the number of teacher absences was out of control, and the teacher did not think twice about missing days at work.

I believe that 30 percent of a great teacher is better than 100 percent of a substitute any day. Substitute teachers have no vested investment nor interest in the success of the classroom that they are subbing. A campus had to be created where our teachers felt celebrated, rewarded, and valued. But first, we had to focus on the students. The decision was made to focus on the students, and he would focus on the staff.

That evening I went back to my hotel and disaggregated the data to see how many students were engaged in sports, band, theater, choir, or other school organizations. To my amazement, over 65 percent of the student body did not participate in anything on campus. A plan was developed that would later become the 2 x 2 x 2 initiative. The 2 x 2 x 2 initiative's goal would be to create a list of all students not currently involved in school activities of any sort. Next, each teacher would have to pick two students from our campus and speak to them twice a day for two months and two different environments. No teacher could have the same student, plus each teacher had to ensure that they spoke to that student about something other than schoolwork. For the next two months, teachers had to ensure they spoke with their students. They speak with the student either in the hallway, stop-by to the classroom, in the cafeteria and/or at the beginning or end of each day. Each teacher also had to communicate with the students in two different ways. For example, a teacher could speak with the student, but that teacher also had to reach a student via a phone call to parents or a handwritten letter to parents telling parents what an honor it was to have their child at school. This initiative allowed teachers to build relationships with not only their students but the parents as well. And there are two things that we know for sure. First, our parents are vital to our student's success, and second, nothing impacts our student's success more than having parents involved in the child's education. The 2 x 2 x 2 initiative accomplishes both things and builds stronger teacher/student relationships in the process.

In the beginning, this was quite uncomfortable for both teachers and students. However, by the end of the first month, student attendance was over 92 percent, and for the first time in several years, there were no teacher absences recorded during the first month of school. By the end of the first six weeks, student attendance was at 95 percent, and the student passing rate had increased by 10 percent. By the end of the second month, many relationships have been formed, and their name knew students, 20 percent of the students had joined a school organization or club (sponsored by the teacher connected with them). Student engagement was at an all-time high.

By the end of the year, the district experienced historical success across all campuses, and all we did was create a platform to build relationships. There was no change in instructional practices; we did not make changes to the curriculum nor bring in any new programs. Our focus was on people, not programs, building relationships, and not focusing on solutions before validating the problem.

Davis's Relationship Model
For Educators

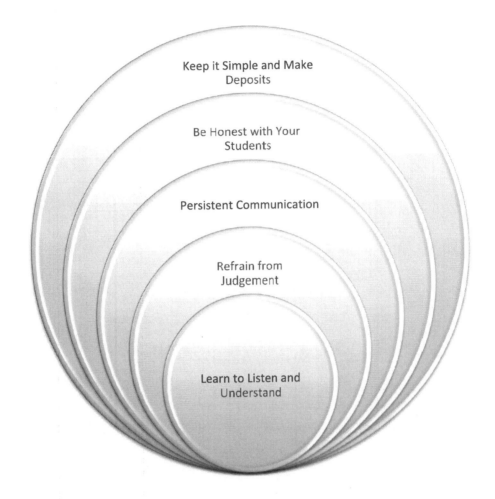

Keep it Simple and Make Deposits

Be Honest with Your Students

Persistent Communication

Refrain from Judgement

Learn to Listen and Understand

Davis's Relationship Model for Educators

1. **Learn to Listen and Understand**: "You never listen" could be the national motto for every student in America. When a student is sent to the office, one of the first things they say is, "the teacher never listens to anything anyone has to say. They just yell and tell you to get out". Is this a problem? It could be however; the solution is simple; just hear them out! When building structure and transparency with a student, (a) connect with them, listen, and understand. (b) hear what they have to say without interrupting or judging (c) focus on what they are saying before making up your mind on what you will do and (d) use empathy and your better judgment. This will go a long way towards building continuous relationships. This is also relationship 101!

2. **Refrain from Judgement**: Work with the student to process and offer suggestions, ideas, and solutions before you give yours. Genuinely hold off on your thoughts until after you have considered theirs. Can you do this with every student in every situation? Of course not, but we are not talking about the extreme and the egregious.

3. **Persistent Communication**: Communicate your expectation, goals, and outcomes persistently, clearly, and in multiple ways and media. Over-communicate these things to your students constantly up to the moment that they become the norm. But even then, we must schedule tune-up time to ensure

everything keeps running smoothly. It is not fair to hold anyone accountable for something that we did not communicate effectively.

4. **Be Honest with Your Students**: If our students hear one thing from us and then see something different, we lose our credibility, and along with our credibility, we also lose their trust. We cannot expect to build relationships without credibility and trust. Often, we fail to tell our students what we expect from them, and then we blame them for not meeting an expectation that was never truly shared with them. When we share our students' expectations, we open the door to dialogue with and further deepen our teacher/student's relationship. *The Heath Brothers state in their book Switch, "what looks like resistance is often a lack of clarity."*

5. **Keep It Simple and Make Deposits**: *Do not over complicate things by having a list of 20 classroom rules.* Show me a teacher that starts the year with a list of 20 classroom rules, and I will show you a teacher that ended the year with a list of 50 classroom rules. Simply say what you mean and avoid using ambiguous language. Making deposits is just that; if we do not deposit something of equal or greater value than what the student is giving, there are no grounds for a relationship. Teachers do not make the mistake of thinking that the lesson you have so thoughtfully planned for today will fulfill the requirements of "equal or greater to your students." Your daily lesson plans are a given to your students; if they did not do anything, your daily lesson plan would still be there.

Davis's Relationship Model for Educators is a student-centered and adult lead model. When we examine the model, as educators master and implement each step of the relationship model, their relationships and relationship potential will increase. By the time an educator has mastered and executed the last component of the model, Davis believes that an educator's relationship capacity will have grown five times since the educator mastered and implemented step one.

Davis's Relationship Model for Educators is an essential part of building relationships and working with our 4-D students. These students have been yelled at to the point that yelling has become their norm. Todd Whitaker said, *"yelling at kids is like mud wrestling a pig; you both get muddy, but only the pig enjoys it"*!

Our 4-D students hope to be cared for and loved in a safe environment with adults they can trust, but they expect to be disappointed. Educators, our 4-D students are waiting for you to go back on your words of not fulfilling your end of the relationship, so they will have reason to disappoint you and misbehave in your classroom. Do not give them the opportunity; give them what they need the most but expect to find the least. Get to know them!

"They may forget what you said, but they will never forget how you made them feel." Carl Buechner

One More Reason to Build Relationships

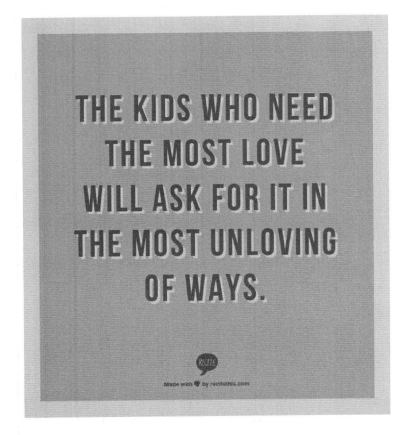

Attitude

Attitude Is Everything

The longer I live, the more I realize the impact of attitude on my life. To me, Attitude is more important than the past than education, than money, than circumstance, than failure, than success, than what other people think, say, or do. It is more important than appearance, giftedness, or

skill. It will make or break a company... a church... a home.

The remarkable thing is, we have a choice every day regarding the attitude we will embrace for that day. We cannot change our past; we cannot change the inevitable. The only thing we can do is play on the one string we have, and that is our attitude...

I am convinced that life is 10 percent what happens to me and 90 percent how I react to it.
And so, it is with you... We oversee our attitudes.

By Charles Swindoll

Every school year, I would hand this out to each one of my students as a teacher. Each copy was signed and dated by me. You think that this was meant for them, but you would be wrong. This was my commitment to my students that I would be mindful of my attitude each day. Think back to the story about Sarah, the freshman student who told me to take my bad attitude and drop it off outside the door. This is one of the reasons Sarah felt confident in what she had to say. Would this be a great tool to use with students in the beginning stages of building relationships? And that is exactly how I used it. Remember, I became a much better teacher once I realized that my students did not owe me anything. This was also my first deposit of something equal or greater in value. This document was my signed sworn word to my students, and believe me, of all the papers that they lost throughout the year – this was not one of them. For most of my students, this was the first time that an adult had taken the time to give them their word and give them formally means to hold that adult accountable.

The Mind:

There are many articles and papers written on the human brain and the human mind. Articles that claim the human brain is capable of 50,000 to 70,000 thoughts a day. This breaks down to about 3,000 views per hour, 50 thoughts per minute, and one thought per second. If we sleep eight hours a day, this number will have to decrease by at least 24,000 thoughts unless they calculate the thoughts that we have while in an unconscious state of mind.

Others have claimed the number of actual thoughts that the human brain is capable of is 12,000, or 15,000 and one of the latest claims is the number is around 20,000 to 29,000 thoughts per day. Either way, this is way too much to think about.

Although none of these articles or papers can definitively say how many thoughts the human brain is capable of, they all agree on one very important point. What is that? That the human brain may be capable of thousands of thoughts per day, but the human brain is only capable of one thought at a time.

It is this one thought that we can control. Our thoughts dictate and control our attitudes.

Select almost any school in America, and we will find a group of teachers whose attitudes are they do not and will not accept late work or find a group of teachers who will accept late work, but they will penalize the student 30 points. Is this a post-secondary attitude being used in our elementary schools, our 6th – 8th-grade campuses, and our high schools, or is this just a teacher who wants to make a statement? In most cases, it is the latter of the two. Each year I have had to listen to teachers, professional educators say to me, "why should I take a student's late work? I have already graded that assignment and posted the grades"? For the educators that take off 30 points, their argument is, "it's not fair to all the students that turned their work in on time." I have written a curriculum in three different school districts in two different states. I have studied part of Common Core and most of Texas's TEKS (Texas Essential Knowledge & Skills), and I have yet to come across a time management component that would support this type of attitude.

When we refuse to accept a student's work, we ensure that a zero will be given for that assignment. Educating students is our only job as educators. How can we successfully educate students when we refuse to accept their work to measure their understanding, mastery, or their lack of clarity of objectives. Why would a student who struggles to make 70 percent each grading period take the time to turn in an assignment knowing that the teacher will take 30 points off before they start to grade? They will not!

This type of attitude is extremely damaging to working with all students, and it is just the environment that our 4-D students become the center of attention. Our attitudes as adults towards our students are far more damaging than we could fathom. Yes, I know that there are many books and data on this topic, and some are best sellers. I guess educators are buying it, just not buying into it, and they are not committing to change.

As an administrator, I committed to focusing on my teachers' behavior and not their attitudes. My goals would always be to make sure my teachers were doing what they needed to do for our students, regardless of their attitudes. My goal was to bring about "cognitive dissonance" with these teachers. Cognitive Dissonance is a mental discomfort experienced by a person that simultaneously holds two or more contradictory beliefs, ideas, or values. Thus, by focusing on the teacher's behavior and having the teacher experience growing student success, by accepting late work and not taking points off late work. At this time, I could say it worked, but in many cases, even though the teacher witnessed firsthand the success of their behavior, they would choose to move on to another campus or district that had a policy for not taking late work from students.

The following is an article that I wrote in 2003.

"Are We Teachers or Judge and Jury?"

I am an administrator in the great state of Texas. As an administrator, I have always had one major pet peeve. That is the "no late work accepted" rule of public-school teachers.

Across the United States, teachers went back to school. Well-rested from summer vacation, pumped up from convocation and motivating keynote speakers. Districts across the U.S. spent millions of dollars to get teachers ready for a new school year, a school year that would show vast improvements in student success in the classroom and on state-mandated tests.

But wait, no one told the teachers that this year we wanted them to teach, not to play the role of

judge and jury. Okay, maybe that is not fair to say about all teachers, so I apologize to most teachers out there. Teachers have prepared their syllabi to show students what is expected of them in the upcoming school year. Unfortunately, some teachers will use their syllabi to create an atmosphere of "I have the power to fail you." Instead of here is how I am going to help you become successful.

61

*As administrators examine their staff members' syllabi, they should be leery of the consequences levied for late work. It is not uncommon for a public-school teacher to boldly print **"NO LATE WORK ACCEPTED."** If not, that statement they levy a harsh penalty for students who turn work in late. Penalties that range from 25 percent off for 1day late up to 50 percent of work one day late.*

What happens if a student turns in the work two days late? Ideally, the students will receive a zero. It does not matter if the students' works reflect a grade worthy of a 100. Because it was late, the judge (teacher) has made his or her ruling (the gavel falls); it is late so let there be consequences. These rules that are not school board policy in most cases do not serve to better our students.

In the public-school system, grades should be ability-based. When a teacher gives a student a

lower grade just because the work was turned in late, this does not reflect that student's ability. Late work could reflect a need for lessons in the organization and/or time management. Both of which any highly qualified teacher could help a student with. A student's academic grade should only reflect his or her ability to grasp and master the curriculum.

When we look at our public schools, we will see an alarming number of student failures. Why, because students are reluctant to make up work when they know it, (1) won't be accepted by the teacher, (2) will meet with stiff penalties, and (3) will not help raise their grade in that class because of the point deductions.

Every teacher reading this article says, "then how do I hold a student responsible for getting work turned in on time"? To those educators, I propose this; let us look at this as an opportunity, not a problem that deserves a consequence. Take this opportunity to get parents involved, note it on their citizenship, or take the opportunity to embrace a teachable moment. Yes, that is what I said as a teachable moment. Is this not why we took on the responsibility of educators? As educators, we need to celebrate the opportunity to teach our students. Here is a novel concept "teachers get paid to teach, grade assignment, and help students grow, not to refuse students work."

As I speak to teachers who embrace this judge mentality, I often ask why they penalize the student for their efforts? The answers are always the same. They range from I, not preparing them for college, to a college professor won't accept late work, or they need to get ready for the real world, and my favorite is they need to know what my expectations are. To these teachers, I would like to say get a clue. Life is predicated on the belief in second chances. I am willing to believe that most of us are where we are because of a second chance.

I would be remiss if I did not mention that I could measure assessment without the student's work; how could one measure assessment? We cannot. If a student has low grades, we can assess where we need to focus on them. If a student has no grades, how can we effectively do our jobs? We have no data by which we can effectively assess the student.

*The concept of "no late work accepted" is the ideology of post-secondary education. Thus, when teachers come into the public-school system, they remember how the statement **"LATE WORK NOT ACCEPTED"** on the professors' syllabi served to motivate them. They forget the other motivating factors such as college cost your money, and not turning your work in would cost you even more money if you had to re-register for that course.*

Our students deserve every teachable moment we have to offer. When a teacher tells a student

because your work is late, I cannot accept it. They create a lifelong impression with that student who says it is late and does not bother trying. At that moment, we set in motion the idea that there is no value in the second effort.

We live in a society that immortalizes the come from behind victory, which embraces the idea that everybody deserves a second chance. So, when we as administrators see these harsh late work rules on our faculty syllabi, did you become an educator to enforce your rules or help students achieve their fullest?

Remember, there are two ways to improve our schools, (1) hire better teachers, and (2) improve the ones we have. We must continuously do both. How are the attitudes of you and your colleagues impacting the student achievement on your campus? Our 4-D students look and focus on the attitudes of teachers. In many instances, they plan their day around our attitudes. Educators, we cannot allow our bad attitudes to nurture the bad attitudes of our students. Procedures, not policies, can be changed with little to no effort. How can we expect to change a child's attitude when we do not desire to change our attitude?

> *"You can't teach children to behave better by making them feel worse. When children feel better, they behave better."* Pam Leo, *Connection Parenting*

In my world there are
NO BAD KIDS,
just impressionable,
conflicted young people
wrestling with
emotions & impulses,
trying to communicate
their
feelings & needs
the only way
they know how.

- Janet Lansbury

What is your attitude about these statements?

In the space provided below, please provide a detailed explanation of your attitude about the quote. Share this quote with two people you work with and listen to their response without comment or judgment.

_____

_____

_____

_____

_____

What do you do as part of your daily practice, that embodies this quote?

_____

_____

_____

_____

_____

EVERY KID IS ONE
CARING ADULT AWAY
FROM BEING A
SUCCESS STORY.

What is your attitude about this statement?

In the space provided below, please provide a detailed explanation of your attitude about the quote. Share this quote with two people you work with and listen to their response without comment or judgment.

_____

_____

_____

_____

_____

What do you do as part of your daily practice that embodies this quote?

_____

_____

_____

_____

_____

A Clean Slate

In my first job out of college, my boss taught me a lesson that has remained with me. Long before education was on my radar, my career started in the fast-food industry. Being young and ready to set the world on fire, no one could tell me anything. A more honest opinion of me back then would be quick to learn with an even quicker temper. Tolerance and forgiveness were not two of my strengths. When one of my workers would waste time, my only reaction was to have them clock out and go home for the day. Once the worker returned to work, that one incident would forever be my opinion of them. My employees did not respect me for this; most of them did not even like me. More employees were calling in sick, missing work, or just quitting on my shift than all the other managers combined. It was almost impossible to get anyone to come in to feel a position when the manager on duty was me.

It was during Wednesday night inventory after we had finished closing up that my manager sat down with me and said to me, "the last thing he wanted was to see was a young talented manager ruin their career because of unrealistic expectations." He went on to say, "this is not the highest paying job, nor is it the destination for most of the people that work here. This is fast food, any one of our cooks, wait for staff, and dishwashers could easily walk next door to Arby', Taco Bell, or across the street to the many fast food places in the area and get a job. In the past three months since you have been my assistant manager, we have experienced more turnover at this time than we have in the past four years. We have had some of my most tenured staff, people who have been with me for six years threaten to quit if I do not get rid of you.

My heart sank; they want me gone. Yes, that is what they said. So, are you firing me? No, but I am going to help you. This is something that should have been addressed when you finished training. What should have been addressed? Should goofing off and coming to work late be acceptable behaviors? Larry, you are missing the point. Everyone will make a mistake from time to time, and we will deal with that at that moment, but when they return to work after their consequence, they do so with a clean slate. He went on to say that once you understand this and start to allow others to have a clean slate, this would give me a clean slate in their eyes. Think about it this way, Larry, that day, and those events are all behind us. Everyone has gone home and went to bed and woke up to a new day. They were punished and, in most cases, have served their consequence. They deserve a clean slate, do you agree. A clean slate, putting things behind us so that we can move forward. Larry, once you have seen the world this way, you realize that carrying a 'dirty' slate around is heavy work. It is a burden to lug along all your shortcomings and screw-ups. It is also a burden to lug along all your preconceptions about other people. And it is even worse to know that others view you

71

through the prism of your previous errors. It kills productivity, and it steals joy.

Our Students Deserve a Clean Slate

Our students, all our students, deserve a clean slate each day of the school year. We do not expect teachers and administrators to have 181 perfect days a year; they will have missed steps and mistakes at some point and time. For them to do their job effectively, we must grant them a clean slate. The ultimate power of a clean slate is that it takes us by the shoulders, turns us toward the future, and gives us a gentle nudge down the road. To accept a fresh start each morning, we must turn from the past, from its shame or disappointment, and even its disciplinary actions toward the next present moment. If we are ever going to change our beliefs, work to build authentic relationships, evolve our attitudes, cultivate student-centered culture and environment where our 4-D students can be successful, we must commit to a clean slate reality.

When we are working with our 4-D students, remember that each day is a new day, and that day brings a clean slate with it. A clean slate is where the real work happens. It is where our 4-D student's success resides; it is where the relationships and learning lives. A clean slate starts with preparing to let go of our fears and chastising to create a new start each day, each class period, and each circumstance. It is where the fun in connecting with our 4-D students truly begins.

It does not matter if it is our defiant, difficult, disrespectful, or disruptive student; we must trust the power of a clean slate. So, wipe our 4-D students' slate, clean, and get started on a new day of giving all students back their joy!

"If a child can't learn the way we teach, maybe we should teach the way they learn!"

Ignacio Estrada

Culture

Two Biggest District and Campus Mistakes

1. Focusing on the "data" before validating the "culture."
2. Building solutions around their "data" without studying their existing "culture".

We must understand that "data" tells us where we are, but our "culture" tells us how we got there. When we expect our data to change for the better without addressing our cultural deficiencies, we should expect to fail. However, year after year, many school districts and schools make this mistake over and over.

History has shown us that the greatest movements have come via "people" not "programs" repeatedly.

Culture:

Currently, everyone wants to compare school culture to the business world. We often hear the phrase if all the schools behave more like businesses. The truth of the matter is when it comes to schools and school districts; we are in the business of educating children and not the education business. There is a difference. My experiences have blessed me to work in both fields, the business field, and 25 years in education. When politicians and business leaders started drawing comparisons between the business world and education, I transitioned from business to education. At first, I would say there is no comparison. But I would be wrong, and I was wrong. Although I still do not agree that business people should lead our education system, I believe there are lessons that we can learn from the business industry. The following is an excellent example of a business that has cultivated a great culture.

Springhill Marriott N. Houston, Texas:

In my travels, I have had the honor of frequenting some of the least expensive, most expensive, not so luxurious to the most luxurious hotels in the US. My stays at hotels have ranged from half a star hotel up to five-star hotels. Hotel prices have ranged in price from $79 a night to the elite resorts at $2,100 a night in my travels. As stated, hotels with water features and hotels with the water just did not work. What makes us come back to a specific hotel or a particular chain of a hotel? Is it the location, the amenities, the price or is it the service?

I am fortunate to be a reward member of several prestigious hotel chains. However, I want to talk about one specific hotel in Houston, Texas. The hotel is the Springhill Marriott in North Houston. My travels have had given me the honor and distinction of staying at this hotel multiple times. It is not the most luxurious hotel; it is not the fanciest hotel, nor is it the most expensive hotel, and the breakfast here is average. The one thing that keeps me coming back to this hotel is the service. What makes the service here so great, and what makes a service here so different? What is it about the service that even makes you notice? It would be easy to say it is the staff, it is the management, or we can chalk it up to the clientele. Let me address the clientele. After staying at this location on several different occasions, I realized it would not matter what clientele they served. Honestly, they treat every client, every guest, and every patron great.

One morning while having breakfast, I noticed the staff standing in the hallway. When I say staff, I mean the hotel manager, his assistant manager, the front desk clerk, the maintenance people, the breakfast personnel, and the hotel's cleaning staff. The first time I noticed this, I thought to myself, "there must be a problem." However, upon further observation, I noticed the staff was cheering, talking about each other, offering suggestions to management, and listening to the management staff. As I finished my breakfast that morning, I left thinking about what an interesting moment? The next day while having breakfast, I noticed a staff meeting in the same area once again. Everyone at the meeting was smiling, enjoying themselves; they reached out at the end of the meeting and cheer. This caused me to start thinking about my stay at the hotel. Had I had any bad experiences there, no. Was there anything different about my stay at this hotel? Were there any subtleties in the service they were providing to me that I had overlooked? I really need to do more research, so I booked the hotel on my next trip to Houston.

For the next several months, I booked a room at this hotel. Every morning my breakfast would be eaten at the same table 9, if available) to observe the morning meetings. Like clockwork every morning, all the hotel staff met in the hallway by the front desk and conducted a standing meeting. My goal was to pay attention to the small things, like the things they said during check-in, how the staff interacted with the clientele during their stay, what foods were new to the breakfast bar, and what was noted during checkout. The next day, I decided to make a request. As I checked in, the front desk clerk asked if there was anything that today can-do Mr. Davis? I responded I would love to have firmer pillows in my room. He smiled at me and continued to check me into the hotel. As I am going into my room, a staff member was walking out. As we passed each other in the doorway, she replied, "Mr. Davis, I brought you some new pillows; I hope that they are firm enough for you; if not, please let the front desk know, and I will bring you more."

The next morning while at breakfast, I asked the breakfast lady if they ever serve chicken sausage? I continued with my normal breakfast oatmeal with raisins, cranberries, and walnuts, grabbed my morning cup of coffee and a slice of whole-grain toast. Again, I sat in the same place at the same table and observed the morning meeting. As the manager started the meeting, I noticed that the young lady I asked about the breakfast sausage commented. The comment was not clear to me; however, this is not unusual during their meetings'; everyone usually spoke. After finishing breakfast, I went about my day. The next day I would be checking out of the hotel and heading back home. As I started to prepare my normal breakfast oatmeal with raisins, cranberries, and walnuts whole-grain toast and a cup of coffee, I noticed on the breakfast bar there they were, chicken sausage. As I finished pouring my coffee cup, the young lady walked over to me and asked if I had noticed the chicken sausage on the breakfast bar? My smile said yes, thank you so much. The young lady was pleased by my response, and she said, you're very welcome.

Upon my next visit to Houston, I chose to stay at the Springhill Marriott in North Houston. By now, the staff knew me by name, and they knew my face. As I entered the hotel, the manager said, welcome back, Mr. Davis; your room is ready, and we have firm pillows waiting for you. My smile and laugh were confirmation that I was pleased. This time I took a moment to ask him about the morning meetings that I had been witnessing the last several months. My question was simple: I noticed that every morning at the same time in the same place in the hallway, there is a meeting. Is it possible for you to tell me what the meeting is about and why you hold them in the same area each time? The manager smiled and said, it is simple, Mr. Davis, it is about culture. The meetings we conduct every morning are called "Stand." We stand in the hallway near the front desk in the breakfast area's eyesight to take care of customers. We host the meetings here to be close to the front desk if someone needs to check-in and/or out, and we are also in the eyesight of the breakfast if a customer or client needs help. This is our moment to share with the staff any customer complaints, compliments, and recognize the works of staff members and mention any customer requests that may have been made. In fact, on your last visit, one of our staff members shared with us that you would like to have chicken sausage on the breakfast bar. Do you remember that? Yes! The manager went on to say that he had been with the Marriott for many years, and during that time, they had undergone different leadership changes. In his many years with the company, the one thing that he valued most was the "Stand" meetings. The "Stand" meetings were a great way to build team morale and cover the day's agenda to shape its culture. Not every staff member had always been committed to the stand meetings, but most of the staff's commitment had been enough to cultivate the culture that the organization was looking for. As for the few staff members, they did not commit to the "Stand" meetings; they would either connect over time and, in some cases, resign for other opportunities.

The manager wanted to share that the staff they inherited and the hotels they took over often were problem areas within the organization. He had never taken over a hotel and the staff intending to fire people or make wholesale changes. The Stand Meetings have been a major contributing factor to his success with the company and his staff and hotel's recognition over the years.

At the end of our conversation, I asked the manager if it would be okay if I stood in the next morning meeting? The manager informed me that it would be unlikely that I will be able to stand in because these meetings were designated for the staff and management team to share and collaborate about their work environment. Although the conversations in "stand meeting" were never negative about customers or clientele, they were exclusive to the hotel's staff and management team. Graciously, I thanked the hotel manager for sharing the information about the Stand Meetings and again expressed my appreciation for him and his team and the hotel's entire staff.

This hotel is a prime example of what a great culture can do. Think about this: the customers and patron of this hotel come from every walk of life. They have different cultures, different social-economic statuses, different geographical areas, and have different core values. This sounds a lot like a school campus; does it not? Most school campuses cannot control the walks of life our students come from, the cultures that they come from, their social-economic background and/or the community a geographic region that they were brought up in. The same issues, concerns, and challenges existed for this hotel. However, the manager here chose to create a culture where excellence would be cultivated instead of blaming the customer, the clientele, or the patrons for these issues. The race, the color, the ethnicity, and/or the religious background of his patrons did not matter to the management team or the hotel staff. Because they created such an inviting and superior culture, every person who booked a room at this hotel treated the staff and the hotel with respect.

The Springhill Marriott on I 45 in North Houston, Texas, is a perfect example of what happens when you create and cultivate a commitment to organizational culture with every team member. Through setting standards, recognizing staff, rewarding publicly outstanding customer service, and giving your team a voice that makes them feel like a valued part of the organization and team.

The Stand Meetings that the staff and management utilize daily to increase the organization's success are the Agile Meeting. On the pages to follow, I want to illustrate two different types of agile meetings. Both of which would increase and foster stronger cultures on a school campus.

Illustration I:

Key Principles of Agile Methodology

Daily Planning is a project planning method that estimates work using self-contained work units called iterations or sprints. Sprints are periods of 1-3 weeks in which a team focuses on a small set of work items and aims to complete them. Agile planning defines which items are done in each sprint and creates a repeatable process to help teams learn how much they can achieve. What did I do yesterday? What will I do today? Or what is stopping me?

Iteration Planning: is an event where all team members determine how much of the Team Backlog, they can commit to delivering during an upcoming Iteration. ... The iteration backlog, consisting of the stories committed to the iteration, with clearly defined acceptance criteria. Stories, Tasks, Definition of

Done, the repetition of a process is part of the fabric of your daily culture.

Released Planning is an approach to product management that considers the intangible and flexible nature; as part of this approach, teams plan iterative sprints across incremental releases: team Capacity, Stories, Priority Size, Definition of Done.

Product Roadmap: Create a vivid picture of your vision for the future. Then set the goals and initiatives that you plan on achieving. Do SWOT analysis, articulate value proposition, capture business models, and more with prebuilt strategy templates. Your team will be aligned and able to maintain a clear focus.

Imagine if every school in the country started their day off with this type of meeting?

Product Vision describes the purpose of a Product, the intention, and aims for customers and users. Having a clear and inspiring Product vision helps motivate and inspire people, like the Development Team, the stakeholders and customers, and users. What, Who, Why, When, Constraints, Assumptions.

Illustration II:

Key Principles of a Campus Agile:

1. **Face to Face Conversations**: With who? Every teacher, paraprofessional, and the administrator must take part in the morning meetings.

2. **Needs Change, So Does Our Culture**: Focused timelines to discuss, measure, and adjust our current campus culture structure.

3. **Working Culture Structure is Measure of Success**: What Cultural practices are working best, and what measurements are we using to determine our success.

4. **Simplicity is Vital**: You must covey assessments, communication, measurements, and adjustments in its simplest form.

5. **Cultural Updates Delivered Regularly**: We must create regular meeting times and hold ourselves accountable for adhering to these meeting times to ensure the regular transference of updated information.

6. **Active User Involvement is Unavoidable**: This means everyone on the campus must participate and be actively involved. I must add constructively involved.

7. **Growing with Growth**: We will strengthen our campus culture through the sharing of our campus success. We will grow by asking and answering the following questions:

   a. What do we do great? How do we make what we are great at second nature?

   b. What are we good at? How do we become great at what we are good at?

   c. What are we not doing well? How do we get better?

Illustration III:

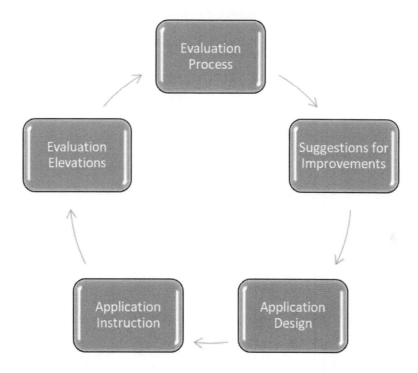

1. **Evaluation of Processes and Current Structures of the Campus:** What is the state of our current campus culture? Where are our high need areas? What should be our top priorities? Remember, this involves every teacher, paraprofessional, and administrator on campus.

2. **Suggestions for Improvement and Process Optimization:** Optimize the process with the ideal combination of strategies. Do we need to build a vibrant campus culture where all our students will be successful?

3. **Application Design Together with the Staff:** We choose the campus strategies, and we review strategies with the

entire staff. The whole staff is part of the process from the beginning, and their feedback is vital.

4. **Application Instruction and Implementation:** Weekly or daily delivery of data from our staff based on the implementation, success, and adjustments of our strategies. Ideally, we allow our staff to lead these meetings and be very mindful of their sharing information.

5. **Evaluation and Elevations:** This is where we determine what our data is telling us, adjust, and celebrate all the milestones that we have accomplished. This is also our opportunity to elevate our campus culture.

Shaping School Culture:

In the book shaping school culture by Deal and Peterson, they take it one step further. They use culture and compare the military, the business world, and our education system. They mention a book "Making the Corps, by Thomas Ricks 1997" pointing to culture as a symbiotic glue that is bonded the Corps together throughout its heralded military campaign. Ricks says culture-that is that the values and assumptions that shape its members are all that the Marines have. It is what holds them together. They are the smallest of US military service and, in some ways, the most interesting. The Marines have the richest culture: formalistic, insular, elitist, with a deep anchor in their history and mythology. I need to point out that I am not saying our schools should run like the military. Simply, I am pointing out that when we define and establish our culture, this culture sets the standard for our values, our assumptions that will then shape our campuses. To better illustrate this point, as educators, we could tour 25 different school campuses within the same school district and likely observe 25 different campus cultures. It is with this understanding that I truly believe that there are no traditionally bad schools. However, there are school cultures that have been traditionally poorly cultivated and traditionally neglected. This tradition of neglect and poor cultivation then becomes systemic throughout the building, staff, and the community. When we look at what is considered a traditionally or historically problem campus, we hear people say, "that it hasn't always been this way." In many instances, faculty, staff, and the community will often point out the moment and time and the leadership that brought about this negative change.

Willard Waller wrote in 1932: "schools have a culture that is their own. There are complex rituals of personal relationships in the schools, a set of folkways, mores, and irrational sanctions, a moral code based upon them. There are games, sublimated wars, teams, and an elaborate set of ceremonies concerning them. Traditions and traditionalists are waiting for their world-old battles against innovators." In Willard Waller's description, if we were to replace the word school with the word business organization, one would begin to easily see the comparisons.

Authors Deal and Peterson state, "Beneath the conscious awareness of everyday school life, there is a stream of thought and activity. This underground flow of feeling and folkways wends its way within schools, dragging people, programs, and ideas towards often unstated purposes: this invisible, taken for the granted flow of beliefs and assumptions gives meaning to what people say and do. It shapes how they interpret hundreds of daily transactions. This deeper structure of life in organizations is reflected and transmitted through symbolic language expressive actions. Culture consists of the stable, underlying social meetings that shake beliefs and behaviors over time."

My First Teaching Position:

My teaching career began in August 1999. Before the first day of class, the campus principal met with me one-on-one. First, I want to thank you for becoming a part of the team, and secondly, he warned me about hanging out in the teachers' lounge. My memory recalls his exact words, "Mr. Davis, I believe in respecting each member of my staff, every teacher, every administrator, every counselor, and each adult that works on this campus. I believe in the work that we do for children above all things on this campus. My advice to you is to get to know your students yourself. Therefore, I am asking you not to hang out in the teachers' lounge. The teachers' lounge is often a place where war stories about our students take place. Now, this is not something that I condone or encourage; it is something that takes place on most school campuses. Throughout the year, you will always hear me address these types of conversations, asking our teachers not to conduct themselves professionally. It is not fair that a teacher should negatively experience a student's reputation through gossip with other teachers. Mr. Davis, I honestly believe when teachers conduct themselves in this manner, this is nothing more than bullying."

Culture fosters school effectiveness and productivity (Purkey and Smith, 1983; Levine and Lizotte, 1990; Newmann and Associates, 1996). Teachers can succeed in a culture focused on productivity (rather than on our ease of work), performance (hard work, dedication, perseverance), and improvement (continuous fine-tuning and refinement of teaching). Such a culture helps teachers overcome their work (Lortie, 1975) by providing focus and collegiality. It provides social motivation to persevere in the demanding work of teaching 30 children in a small space.

School culture affects every part of the enterprise, from what faculty talks about in the lunchroom to the types of instruction valued, to the way professional development is viewed, to the importance of learning for all students. Strong positive collaborative cultures have potent effects on many features of schools. "Shaping School Culture" (Terrence E. Deal and Kent D. Peterson, 1999).

Environment

Many of us struggle with the understanding of the difference between "culture" and "environment." When I present to educators at conferences and during workshops, I explain it this way; "culture is the content and environment is the context in which everything takes place." Others have explained the difference in this way; "Culture is a human feature. It describes our culture, food, traditions, music, and art. The *environment is a physical feature.* It describes trees, grasslands, fertile soil lands, desserts, and things like that." Since we have already discussed culture in the earlier portion of the book, we will now examine the "environment."

> *"Our job is to teach the students we have.*
> *Not the ones we would like to have.*
> *Not the ones we used to have.*
> *Those we have right now.*
> *All of them.*
> Dr. Kevin Maxwell

Mr. Johnson's 5th Period Class:

It is 1:20 pm. Mr. Johnson's 5th-period history class is just about to start. The tardy bell rings, and the students are still walking through the door. Mr. Johnson is at his usual spot during passing periods and the beginning of each class, "his desk." As the tardy bell stops ringing and several students casually walk into the class, the rest of the students engage in conversation other than history. As you look around the classroom, you notice that the following items are nowhere to be found:

- There is not a bell ringer on the board
- The Daily Lesson Plan is not framed on the board.
- The closing of the lesson.
- No classroom expectations.
- No data Information is posted anywhere.
- No student work is posted in the classroom.
- No School Spirit or School Pride Board.
- There does not appear to be any order for starting class.

The students continue to talk amongst themselves for the first ten minutes of a 55-minute class. At this point, Mr. Johnson starts to take attendance. He must call out each student's name because there is not a seating chart. Also, because the students are all talking, Mr. Johnson must call each student's name multiple times. Taking class attendance should take minutes, but the apparent lack of structure taking attendance has taken up another 5 minutes of academic time.

Mr. Johnson finally finishes taking attendance, and he is now trying to call the class to orders; this process takes another 5 minutes of academic time. Let us review our lost time:

- Ten minutes of students being off task.

- Five minutes to take class attendance.
- Five minutes to call the class to order.
  - This is 20 minutes of academic time lost in a 55-minute class

Mr. Johnson has finally got the attention of the classroom. He starts to speak with the class about their most recent exam.

"I have here in my hands the results of your last test. I am very disappointed with the results; it appears that even after applying a curve, only a few of you passed the exam. So, I have decided to throw out this exam and try and figure out what it is that you did not get. I know that I taught you all the important information you should have needed for this exam, but I cannot figure out why you did not know it. I am going to go over all the objectives that we covered for our last units. For the next 25 minutes of class, Mr. Johnson starts to cover all the previous units' objectives. As Mr. Johnson covers the objectives, his students sit in rows, listen to music, talk, some are on their phones, and a few students listen to him.

The students in Mr. Johnson's class have realized that if they keep their distractions down to a minimum that the teacher will continue with his teaching. As Mr. Johnson continues to do what he believes to be re-teaching, he never checks for engagement. Mr. Johnson had mastered the art of teaching through all distractions, mostly minor distractions. Mr. Johnson is now preparing to ask questions to do what he believes to be checking for understanding. He asks one question after another to students that never answer his questions. When students fail to answer his questions, Mr. Johnson will give the students the answers. Then he will move on to the next questions. This routine continues without having students take notes, redirecting the off-task students back to the task, and having only a handful of students answer a handful of questions.

With 10 minutes left in the 5th-period, Mr. Johnson instructs students to get their things together and prepare to move to the next class. For the next 10 minutes, the students in Mr. Johnson's class talk, listen to music and play on their phones. Mr. Johnson goes back to his desk and logs onto his computer. Data tells us that students are most prepared to learn the first 10 minutes and the last 10 minutes of academic time. As we look back on time spent in Mr. Johnson's class, the first 20 minutes of class was spent off task and disconnected from learning, and the last 10 minutes were wasted once again, allowing students to be unengaged in learning. The 25 minutes Mr. Johnson used for the academic time was spent with most of the class disconnected from a highly ineffective learning environment. Now, as the bell rings to dismiss from 5th-period and transition to 6th-period, Mr. Johnson students have sat in a non-learning climate for the last 10 minutes and will spend a six-minute passing period moving their 6th-period class where they will enter mentally not ready to learn.

The Passing Period:

As students start to transition from 5th-period to 6th-period, we see group after group of students standing around talking and not moving to their next class. We also see groups of students involved in PDA (Public Displays of Affection) where most teachers constantly look the other way, so they will not have to address the students. Some students are blocking the way so that other students cannot get to their next class. As we look around, we see very few adults supervising the transition of students during this time. Only a few teachers are standing in the hallway, ushering students to their next class, and very few teachers standing at their doorway greeting and inviting students into their classrooms. Most students are not even attempting to move towards their 6th-period class for the first 5 minutes of the passing period; it is not until the one-minute warning bell rings before most students start to head to class. However, there are still many students that continue to linger in the hallway. **P.E. Class:**

The P.E. classroom should offer students another opportunity for structure and organization within their school day. Upon visiting the P.E. classroom, you observe students sitting in the bleachers and not dressed for physical education. The coaches are divided; some sat around talking to each other, some in the locker room, and some are off campus. This has become the norm and the daily routine for the student and coaches every day.

Each P.E. class period that this behavior can persist is placing further strain on the entire campus environment. We should be asking how campus administrators allow a group of educators to collect a paycheck and not do their jobs. Some may be thinking that it is only P.E., and some would be wrong. Every class and every teacher contribute to our campus environment. When students become accustomed to going to a learning environment where learning is not the expectation or the norm, it will promote off-task behavior in classrooms with high expectations.

Organizations spend millions of dollars on administrative retreats, where they develop their vision and mission statements. They spend even more time on devising and creating marketing materials to display their vision and mission statements. School districts post their vision and mission statements on the district website and district stationery. The district superintendent talks about the district's vision and mission at convocation and back to school in-service. Teachers, paraprofessionals, counselors, campus administrators, and central office personnel all stand and cheer with excitement. But when you step inside the walls of most of these organizations or campuses, you rarely observe an environment that embodies the vision and mission that they boast of being about.

Six Traits of an Effective Learning Environment:

1. We love our students.
2. Students are safe, loved, celebrated, and they matter.
3. Administrators, educators, and staff strive for student success.
4. Teachers work with students and parents, and administrators to work for students, parents, and teachers.
5. Student errors and mistakes are opportunities to improve and become better.
6. The campus uses feedback and data to improve learning.

The role of a "great teacher" is not to give greatness to their students and colleagues but to help bring out the greatness that lies inside every child. Bethany Hill says, "every child that you pass in the hall has a story that needs to be heard. Maybe you are the one meant to hear it". Imagine an environment where students had a voice, and adults were eager to listen. This is an effective learning environment. I suggest these ten things should be a part of an effective student-centered learning environment.

1. Tell and/or show our students that we love them every day.
2. Focus on and acknowledge our students doing things right.
3. Do something that demonstrates to our students that we value them.
4. Teach them how valuable they truly are.
5. Recognize, reward, and praise our students for their work and their contributions to our campus.
6. Sponsor a club or organization and attend sporting and social events to support our students.
7. Continuously building foundations for trust where our students want to share with us.
8. Recognize how hard our students work and make connections between their hard work and their success.
9. Let our students know how grateful we are that they are on our campus and in our classes.
10. Let our students know just how happy you are to be a part of their education. Our students deserve to see educators and adults that smile and enjoy working for them each day.

When their teachers know them, students come to school, connected to the campus, and engaged in their work. This is the type of environment that students will flourish academically, athletically, artistically, and socially. When we praise students, it goes to their heads. But when we criticize or belittle them, it goes to their heart. Taking learning to the heart is what we want all our students to do. It will only happen if we as educators take teaching and our craft to heart as well.

A Model Environment for All Students

"Especially Our 4-D Students."

Purpose: To teach students to make responsible choices.

Focus: To learn from the outcomes of their decisions.

Objectives:

- Intentional
- Internal Focus
- Done by the student
- Logical or natural
- Soft Skills
- Respectful two-way communication

Examples:

- Developing a plan describing how you will behave without violating the expectations when you are in a similar situation.
- Practicing appropriate behavior in a private meeting with the teacher.
- Student developed a classroom mission statement of student expectations written by the students with input from the teacher. Posted in the classroom and signed by students and teachers.

Student learns ...

- I cause my outcomes (ownership of their behavior).
- I have more than one alternative behavior in any situation.
- I have the power to choose the best alternative.

Connection, Competence & Control: Teacher Commitment

Connection:

- Every day I will be at the door to greet each student.
- I will ask for the opinion of at least two students who rarely contribute.
- I will invite two tough students to lead a class discussion at least once during class.

Competence:

- At least twice this week, I will help _____, _____, _____, and _____ (four of my lowest performing students) to earn A's by comparing their current work to their past work if they make an academic improvement.

- I will give the class at least two open-book quizzes at the beginning of class so that all students on time with their book can earn A's.

- I will give each student at least one opportunity (every six weeks) to redo, revise, or retake a major assignment or test to improve their six week's grades.

- I will establish a late work policy that will not include a reduction in point for all my students; ex. Late work must be turned in within 3 class days of the original due date.

- I will recognize all achievements by my students no matter how small; example, James turns in a homework assignment for the first time these six weeks. Genuine recognition without sarcasm.

Control:
- I will give meaningful choices within each assignment to all students.

- If a difficult student breaks a rule, before I decide on a consequence, I will first ask the student what could help the student not break the rule again. I will do this at least two times.

- I will invite a difficult student to solve either a class or school problem involving challenging behavior.

Working with Our 4-D Students:
Preventions:
What can be done to prevent discipline problems?
1. Know & express yourself clearly.
2. Know your students.
3. Make your classroom a motivating place.
4. Teach responsibility and caring.
5. Establish effective rules and consequences.
6. Keep yourself current.

7. Deal with stressful conflict.

Actions:

What to do when discipline problems Occur:

1. Stop the misbehavior quickly.
2. Get back to teaching.
3. Keep students in the class (whenever possible).
4. Implement consequences.
5. Collect Data.

Resolutions:

Find what is needed to prevent another problem:

1. Develop a mutually agreeable plan with the student (whenever possible).
2. Implement the plan.
3. Monitor plan/revise if necessary.
4. Use creative/unconventional approaches when necessary (unconventional... see administrator).

> *"I want students to be able to say these things when they leave me:*
> *I am a worthwhile person; I deserve a place on this earth:*
> *I am successful; I am ready for whatever the world throws at me – today or tomorrow."*
> *Robert Ford*

What are your thoughts on this statement?

In the space provided below, please provide a detailed explanation of your thoughts about the quote. Share this quote with two people you work with and listen to their response without comment or judgment.

_____

_____

_____

_____

_____

What do you do as part of your daily practice that embodies this quote?

_____

_____

_____

_____

_____

What Every Educator Should Know About Every Student

If we only look at our students' surface, then we are guilty of missing out on 90 percent of who our students really are. As you review the picture below and we can start to see all the factors that contribute to our students' make-up! As we go through the strategies for working with our 4-D students, I want you to reference the chart below when working with your 4-D students.

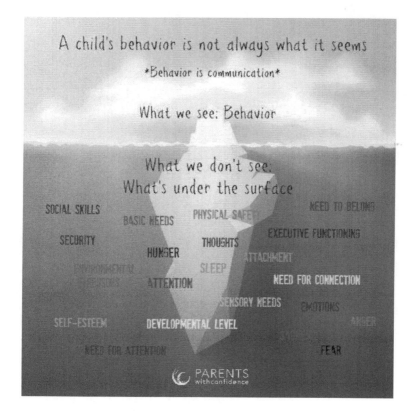

103

B.R.A.C.E. Yourself

We are here to discuss our 4-D (defiant, difficult, disrespectful, and disruptive) students. When we talk about our 4-D students, are we talking about one student that falls into all four categories, or are we talking about a different student that falls into each category? Think about your 4-D students and write down strategies based on beliefs, relationships, attitude, culture, and environment you feel would work best for you. Work with your campus members as a team and develop a list of campus-wide strategies to use throughout your campus.

Simple Truths:

Teachers are people, too; they are not emotionless robots. This is a fact that I know better than most. I had more names other than the one my parents gave me at birth more times than I can remember in my career. The key for me was that I never took anything any student said personally. Our students will often stoop to disruptive behavior and/or public outbreaks because they have never been taught coping skills to deal with conflict. Often their behavior is coming from a deep place of hurt and unseen scars.

I have had to deal with three prevailing challenges in my experience with our 4-D students.

The first one is the educators' perception of the students' ability to achieve and behave accordingly. When we stop making excuses about why certain students cannot behave and contribute to our schools and classrooms and focus on our beliefs, relationships, attitudes, cultures, and environment, they will succeed. We must meet our students where they are and take them to where they need to be. When we provide students with high quality focused instruction, we begin to remove our barrier to success. The second one is that we have students who we believe to be a 4-D student; they still have the cognitive ability to learn and grow emotionally and mentally. The third one care enough as teachers not to allow our students to make excuses for not being successful. Whenever we raise the bar, our students find ways to climb over it, but when we lower that same bar, they crawl under it.

"I've never once met a child who can't come to deep levels of healing if you understand what they need." Dr. Karyn Purvis

Simple Reminders

1. Refused to accept excuses and stop making them ourselves.
2. Legitimize misbehavior that you cannot stop; if you have daily paper airplane flights buzzing past you, take five minutes to have a paper airplane contest.

3. Use a variety of ways to communicate with children. (sticky notes, handwritten notes, one on one). Communicate on our time when possible making their time important to us. This should be used to convey positive messages, as well.

4. Be responsible for ourselves and allow children to take responsibility for themselves.

5. Realize that you will not reach every child **"but act as if you can."**

6. Start fresh every day: "What happened yesterday is finished. Today is a new day."

7. Dealing with student behavior is part of the job.

8. Always treat students with dignity.

9. Discipline works best when integrated with effective teaching practices.

10. Acting out is sometimes an act of sanity (when children act out, they provide feedback to the teacher).

Important Reminders

1. In a student/teacher interaction – we are the adult

2. In a student/parent/teacher interaction – we are the professional

3. Document do not dwell

4. Our memories produce our outlook on people and in life

5. Teachers are not entitled to have a bad day
   o One bad day out of 30 is all that students and parents will remember.

- o Thirty percent of a teacher on their worst day is better than 100 percent substitute any day.
- o Ninety-three percent of our students never cause issues in our classrooms.

Facts and Myths about 4-D Students

(Fact) They have been "yelled" at enough. Our yelling means nothing to them; our 4-D students expect to be yelled at. Thus, surprise them with a gentle calmness.

(Fact) They have been threatened enough. Our threats offer them the opportunity to see if the action is worth the threatened outcome

(Fact) They have been judged enough. They are expecting to be judged negatively by adults.

(Fact) They value peer acknowledgment over adults. It is a defense mechanism.

(Myth) If I ignore the behavior, they will eventually stop

(Myth) If I could just get this student out of my class, both of us would be better off!

The fact is, only the teacher will be better off. When we subscribe to this type of thinking, we further supported the students' belief that acting out is the way out, and the next teacher has less of an opportunity to dispel that belief.

107

"Almost every student you meet may be fighting a battle you know nothing about. Stop, Think, then make your response accordingly." Robert John Meehan

The Halo Effect

Before we get started with a list of proven and suggested strategies that we can implement as part of our daily routine, I want to mention one more trap that is an easy one for educators to fall into. This trap is called "The Halo Effect."

The halo effect is a type of cognitive bias_in which our overall impression of a person influences how we feel and think about their character. Essentially, your overall impression of a person ("He is nice!") impacts your evaluations of that person's specific traits ("He is also smart!"). *(Standing, L. G., in The SAGE Encyclopedia of Social Science Research Methods, Volume 1, 2004)*

A perfect example of the halo effect in our classrooms is when a student that teachers have deemed a "good student" can never do anything wrong. This student benefits from the doubt about missing assignments and/or being tardy to class. In this same scenario, a student deemed a bad student will never reap that same benefit when it comes to missing assignments and late to class.

"Strong teachers don't teach content.

Google has content.

Strong teaching connects learning in ways that

Inspire kids to learn more and strive for greatness."

Eric Jens

"Who Are You Talking About"?
Generation Z

In 2006 the United States experienced a record number of births. This birth boom (not to be confused with the "Baby Boomers" of 1946) will eventually change America's landscape. Here are some interesting and key facts about the students sitting in front of us every day.

- Forty-nine percent of these births were Hispanic
- Gen-Z represent about 25 percent of the United States population
- In 20 years, Gen-Z will be the largest population in our workforce
- Four age groups now.
  - Young Adult (19-22 years old)
  - Teens (13-18 years old)
  - Tweens (8-12 years old)
  - Toddler/Elementary school age
- With the advent of computers and web-based learning, children leave toys at a younger age. This is referred to as KGOY - Kids Growing Older Younger. Companies are suffering, i.e., Mattel (Barbie dolls); in 1990s average

target market child was ten years old, in 2000, it dropped to 3 years old.

- o Generation Z has grown up in an era of technology. Technology has been integral to the type of toys they play with, how they communicate, what gets their attention, what engages them, and yes, what is important to them.
- Sixty-one percent of children 8-17 have televisions in their rooms; 35 percent have video games.
  - o 4 million will have cell phones

- Motivated by social rewards, mentorships, and constant feedback

- Public ridicule, sarcasm, verbal challenges, and/or public displays of discipline does not go over well with the Gen-Z population
- Like experiential rewards for personal growth, o Experience is the best teacher (not really, but this explains why their actions and deeds will always outweigh any punitive action that we may have)
- Expect structure, clear direction, and transparency o **The Davis Model of Relationships (Steps 1, 3, 4 & 5)** o **Learn to Listen and Understand**: "You never listen" could be the national motto for every student in America. When a student is sent to the office, one of the first things they say is, "the teacher never listens to anything anyone has to say. They just yell and tell you to get out". Is this a problem? It could be however; the solution is simple; just hear them

out! When building structure and transparency with students, (a) connect with them, listen, and understand. (b) hear what they have to say without interrupting or judging (c) focus on what they are saying before making up your mind on what you will do and (d) use empathy and your better judgment. This will go a long way towards building continuous relationships. This is also relationship 101!

- **Persistent Communication**: Communicate your expectations, goals, and outcomes persistently and clearly and in multiple ways and media. Teachers should over-communicate these things to your students on a persistent basis until they become the norm. But even then, we must schedule tune-up time to ensure everything keeps running smoothly. It is not fair to hold anyone accountable for something that we did not communicate effectively.

- **Be Honest with Your Students**: If our students hear one thing from us and then see something different, we lose our credibility, and along with our credibility, we also lose their trust. We cannot expect to build relationships without credibility and trust. Often, we fail to tell our students what we expect from them, and then we blame them for not meeting an expectation that was never genuinely shared with them. When we share our students' expectations, we open the door to dialogue with our students and further deepen our teacher/student relationship. *The Heath Brothers state in their book Switch, "what looks like resistance is often a lack of clarity."*

- **Keep It Simple and Make Deposits**: Do not over complicate things by having a list of 20 classroom rules. Show me a teacher that starts the year with a list of 20 classroom rules, and I will show you a teacher that ended the year with a list of 50 classroom rules. Simply say what you mean and avoid using ambiguous language. Making deposits is just that; if we do not deposit something of equal or greater value than what the student is giving, there are no grounds for a relationship. Teachers do not make the mistake of thinking that the lesson you have so thoughtfully planned for today will fulfill the requirements of "equal or greater to your students." Your daily lesson plans are a given to your students; if they did not do anything, your daily lesson plan would still be there.

- Fifty-three percent prefer face-to-face communication
  o Here is where our opportunity exists

Let us get started.

Defiant Students

1. The definition of defiant is someone or something that resists behaving or conforming to what is asked or expected. (www.yourdictionary.com)

2. Dictionary.com defines defiant as boldly resistant or challenging: a defiant attitude.

3. The Cambridge dictionary defines defiant as "proudly refusing to obey authority" and "not willing to accept criticism or disapproval."

4. Merriam Webster defines defiant as "full of or showing a disposition challenge, resist, or fight – full of or showing impudent behavior."

As an educator, I can agree with each of these definitions. But I want to say that Merriam Webster has been peering into some of our classrooms. Our defiant students appear to come to class each day, looking for a fight or waiting for a fight. Our defiant students appear to be sitting and waiting for their opportunity to defy us. I am here to share with you that this is not the case. Our defiant students are not focused on you as much as they are focused on their schedule and self. As educators, we do not look forward to the class periods that have our defiant children in them.

Our students deserve to have adults standing in front of them each day with a smile on their face. I often reference the song from the Disney movie "Snow White" – Whistle while you work. It is hard to whistle when our faces are in the frown position. Working with our defiant students is tough, it is trying, it is draining, but we can never make it personal.

Defiant children are never fun to deal with. Know that it is a power struggle, and as the instructional leader, you need to come out on top like the one in charge and keep the child's respect at the forefront.

"When children are defiant, their goal is not to annoy, disrespect, or frustrate us," said Margaret Berry Wilson. "Rather, their goal often is to feel significant."

Teachers sometimes get into power struggles with defiant children, says Wilson. "But teachers never win power struggles. Once you are in one, you have lost. And so, has the child: No one wins a power struggle." When power struggles occur in the classroom, two major accomplishments happen. First, every student in the class is deprived of their academic learning because there is no teaching. Secondly, the defiant student has just gotten their way, as all accountability is set aside for the sake of this futile confrontation. In Stephen R. Covey's book "The 7 Habits of Highly Effective People," Mr. Covey's Habit # 4 is "Think Win/Win. When educators engage in a power struggle with students, the win/win concept ceases to exist.

What is the alternative? Orchestrating things to prevent defiance in the first place, says Wilson. If it occurs, it is calmly working with students in ways that address their need to feel significant—while holding them accountable for following the expectations.

How do we work with a student whose defiance ranges from telling me to "shut up" to slamming books on the desk, ignoring my every request, and even giving off threatening glares? As educators, we all have experienced the classic "defiant child." They profess to hate school, has trouble getting along with other students, and frequently disobeys her teacher. What should we do?

Proposed Strategies:

When looking to employ strategies to support and work with any student, it is important to have first made some investment type into that student. The investment could range from knowing some little personal background on the student, having spent time trying to help the child academically and/or simply invested time in speaking to the student from time to time. Defiant students are not usually receptive to the "cold call." The cold call is that phone call that we receive during dinner time trying to convince us that we need to send our hard-earned money to a perfect stranger for something that we do not need. If we have never taken the time to make any good faith deposits in a student, it is extremely hard to approach that student now and have that student believe that you have their best interest at heart.

Thus, these are the proposed strategies that I am giving you, but I urge you to use the strategies that will work best for your student and not the strategy that you feel will work best for you, the educator. Educators are warned against the urge to discount strategy or strategies because you think that "Mr. Davis just doesn't know the students that I have in my class." This cannot be your "belief of attitude" if you truly want to make a difference. Remember, I asked you to B.R.A.C.E. yourself; if we are going to make a difference, we must be willing to think students first and me second.

1. ***Build positive relationships***. Defiant students need to know that you will still care about them no matter what happens. Focus on positive attributes, learn about their interests, and channel those strengths into playing an important role in the classroom. For example, a student might be the expert at fixing the small engine repairs.

Allow the student to make real-world connections about their learning using what they know about small engine repair. *Davis Model step one learn to listen and understand.*

2. ***Reinforce progress and effort.*** Notice and give specific praise for positive, cooperative behaviors, however small. Wilson believes teachers should avoid saying "I like," "I appreciate," and "I want," which convey the idea that it's about pleasing or complying with the teacher rather than doing the right thing. Such language may also make a student feel manipulated. Better to talk about positive results–for example, "When you helped Kevin this morning, I think he felt valued." This is one of the few times that I encourage "I" messages. *Davis Model step three, persistent communication.*

3. ***Teach students how to disagree respectfully.*** "It's empowering for all children–especially those who struggle with authority–to know that they may disagree with adults," said Wilson–as long as it is done appropriately. Students should be taught to use phrases like "I feel that" and "I suggest" when they believe something is unfair or should be changed. This may be the only other "I" message that I encourage. *Davis Model step 2, refrain from judgment.*

4. ***Channel children's energy in positive directions.*** If students are fired up about an issue, they should be encouraged to write letters to the school or community paper, get involved in service projects or do their research

on it. This is a perfect example and opportunity to connect a student to the school community.

5. ***De-escalate defiance***. The goal is to keep the child safe and calm things down. Avoid pushing the student's buttons; do not do anything to heighten stress or invite more resistance. My son was about three years old when he first felt comfortable enough to stand on an elevator. When we stepped onto the elevator, my son started pressing buttons, as many as he could. He pushed as many as six buttons. But none of those buttons stopped us from getting to where we were going. So, it dawned on me that my son could only push the buttons that he could reach. Educators do not let our students have access to your important buttons.

Do not try to reason or make an emotional appeal when the child is too angry to process it.

Slow down. Taking a few minutes before saying anything raises the probability that the child will listen. After the incident, reflect on what the trigger might have been–and do not underestimate the power and influence of what those triggers represent to the student.

6. ***Intervene early***. At the first sign of defiance, set clear limits. The earlier the teacher intervenes, the less likely the child will be to dig in and escalate. Use brief, direct statements, speak in a calm, matter-of-fact voice, avoid

questions, and keep body language neutral. For example, "Andrew, take a seat. You can read or draw for now."

7. ***When using consequences***, offer limited choices. Because students who have escalated to defiance are often seeking power, it is smart to give them a selection of consequences. For example, "Anna, either you can come with us now, or I can have Mrs. Bell come to sit with you. Which do you choose?"

8. ***Avoid negotiating at that moment.*** Once a teacher has decided on a consequence or redirection for a defiant child, it is wise to stick with it. "Negotiating during the incident will invite further testing," said Wilson. "It also sends the message that children can avoid a redirection or consequence by resisting." And do not get into a power struggle. For example, "Chris, we're done talking about that for now. Everyone gets your writing journals out and start on your stories from yesterday."

9. ***Give the child time and space.*** Once a consequence has been given, it is best to step back and give the child space to comply in a reasonable amount of time. Asking for immediate compliance invites further defiance. Allow the student's behavior to dictate your next move; in other words – do not let the "slow compliance" to be confused with "no compliance." The student is doing what you asked them to do and trying to save face simultaneously. Educators focus on the student's behavior, not their attitudes.

Actions That We Must Avoid

The following list is comprised of what I like to call triggers. If we find ourselves using any of the below actions, we guarantee that a struggle will ensue. The below actions will do more to trigger a negative response from our defiant students than it will do to elicit the desired behavior.

Lose your temper (yelling or using sarcasm tend to escalate oppositional kids)

- *Engage in the interaction in front of other students.* As an adult, you need to understand that you are the minority in the classroom and that the student is among their peers' audience.

- *Try to persuade the student or, worse, bribe the student.* When we resort to these actions, we are surrendering our authority to the student.

- *Threaten the student.* Educators, these students have been threatened enough, and one more threat means absolutely nothing to the student. Again, the defiant student is expecting us to react in this manner.

- *Adding more and more consequences.* This reminds me of the movie "The Breakfast Club" when the detention teachers tell the student to stop talking or add more time to his time in detention. What ensues is a power struggle between the teacher and the student, where the student continues to talk back to the teacher, and the teacher

121

continues to add more and more consequence to the student's discipline. So much more that it became impossible for the student to serve out the consequences. Stick to the initial consequence that you decide on and move on.

- ***Trying to embarrass the student or put them down.*** Remember that the student is the majority in the classroom, and the results will not look favorably upon you in this adult/child interaction. If you feel that you got the student's best in this situation, you have just lost every student's respect in your class and their parents. Trust me; these stories travel home with our students.

- ***Not following through with consequences or being inconsistent.*** Keep your word even if you are having second thoughts about the situation. It is far better to be a tough and consistent educator than the educators that students can manipulate into changing their minds.

- ***Letting the struggle go on way too long.*** When we ask the class to quiet down or stop talking, and a student yells out, "I'm not the only one talking." Educators do not acknowledge the comment; just continue with your lesson. If we acknowledge this student comment as leaders of the classroom, we just open the door for the struggle to continue.

- *Crowd the student.* Give students their space and give yourself some wait time. Remember, you are in control of this situation.

- *Get annoyed at every little thing they do wrong...always focus on the big battle.* Educators, if we are at this point with our student, this has become personal to us. We cannot take things personally; as educators, we must have very short memories of student behavior. Document the student's behavior educators, do not dwell on their behavior. Documentation allows us to collect data about the student, and as an educator, we can formulate a plan to support the student.

Practice Scenario's

These are the following scenarios about several defiant students. Read each scenario carefully, and in the space provided after each scenario, write down how you would utilize B.R.A.C.E. to support the student. Please feel free to refer to the Davis Relationship Model for Educators to help you develop your plan.

Defiant Student Dante'

In my first year as a teacher, I encountered an extremely defiant young man. His name is Dante. The week leading up to the start of classes I was told all sorts of stories about Dante. I decided I wanted him to sit right next to me. On the morning of the first day, he came into my room and saw where his seat was and got very upset. He started telling me that he was sure other teachers told me stories about him. He was respectful and not disruptive in any way but refused to sit in that seat.

After several minutes of him refusing to sit at his assigned desk, I pulled him aside. Again, he told me that he was sure I had heard stories about him. I told him that yes, I did hear stories, but they mean nothing to me. I continued to tell him that I did not know him, he has never done anything to me, and he does not know me. This was our chance to get to know each other and having him right next to me would give us better access to each other. The shift of emotion on his face was drastic. He thanked me, walked into the room, and took his assigned seat. He wore it as a badge of honor.

Over that year, we would butt heads several times, but he always came to me when he needed to talk or advice about job applications. He did not make the best choices when he left high school and got arrested on a very serious charge. He contacted me from jail, and we corresponded when he went to prison. Upon his release, he told me that I was the only person in his life who stuck by his side and believed in him. He has applied to a local community college and will be attending this fall.

Defiant Student:

Name: _____ School/Classroom: _____

City: _____ State: _____

How would you use Belief, Relationships, Attitude, Culture & Environment to support this student, and which elements of B.R.A.C.E. would be most beneficial to this student?

_____

_____

_____

_____

_____

_____

_____

_____

_____

Defiant Student Oliver

Oliver is a sixth-grade student from the East Coast who recently transferred to a school in Colorado. Oliver had been expelled from his previous schools for being defiant, refusing to follow any school rules, and disregarding all adults. Oliver is a student that comes to class and waits patiently for the moment to show his defiance. When that moment occurs, Oliver becomes belligerent with the teacher, other students, and administrative staff. In several parent-teacher conferences, Oliver has openly defied his mother and grandmother. Oliver has on more than one occasion told the administrators that his dad has told him that no woman has a right to tell a man what to do. Unfortunately, Oliver's dad does not live in the household with Oliver, his mother, and his grandmother. It was during one of these parent-teacher conferences that it was revealed that his dad was incarcerated.

Defiant Student:

Name: _____ School/Classroom: _____

City: _____ State: _____

How would you use Belief, Relationships, Attitude, Culture & Environment to support this student, and which B.R.A.C.E. elements would be most beneficial to this student?

_____

_____

_____

_____

_____

_____

_____

_____

_____

Defiant Student Kevin

Kevin is a high school student that easily loses his temper when he is redirected, or his behavior is corrected. Kevin argues over every rule in every teachers' classroom. If the teacher asked him to stop talking, he would ignore that teacher and continue talking or make sounds as if the teacher was irritating him and would continue to talk. Kevin was consciously making rude comments to other students and/or inappropriate comments to female students. When the teacher would address these comments, Kevin was starting to argue with the teacher and throw temper tantrums in the middle of the class. Kevin often blamed others for his actions and never took responsibility for anything. Kevin was a unique combination of a defiant, disrespectful, and disruptive student. Kevin did not recognize the authority of any adult on the campus. In speaking with his parents, the Counselor wanted to ask if Kevin had oppositional defiance disorder. The parents informed the school this was not the case that Kevin had been tested for multiple disorders throughout the years.

Defiant Student:

Name: _____ School/Classroom: _____

City: _____ State: _____

How would you use Belief, Relationships, Attitude, Culture & Environment to support this student, and which B.R.A.C.E. elements would be most beneficial to this student?

_____

_____

_____

_____

_____

_____

_____

_____

_____

Defiant Student Johnathan

Jonathan is the quintessential teenager concerned with his reputation, appearance, and approval of his peers than he is with adults. When Jonathan has the attention of his peers, his defiance has been known to reach all-new levels. When an adult attempt to redirect Jonathan's inappropriate behavior or poor choices, he acts out to gain and keep the attention focused on him. As Johnson's audience and attention from his peers grow, so does the amount of his defiance. Jonathan does not care about the consequences of his actions; Jonathan is more concerned with the narrative of the story behind his actions.

Defiant Student:

Name: _____ School/Classroom: _____

City: _____ State: _____

How would you use Belief, Relationships, Attitude, Culture & Environment to support this student, and which elements of B.R.A.C.E. would be most beneficial to this student?

_____

_____

_____

_____

_____

_____

_____

_____

_____

Difficult Student

What does "Difficult" mean to you? Defining the actions of the "difficult" student is not easy to define. A student that we have deemed difficult may be difficult for several reasons. A difficult student could be defiant, disrespectful, or even disruptive, or they may not be any of those things. We must look at our difficult students through a different lens. Again, what does difficult mean to you?

I have had several students that I felt were difficult, and none were defiant, disrespectful, or disruptive. One of my difficult students refused to open up. He was new to the district, and he would come to class, not do his work, and not once did he cause a disturbance. Whenever I would speak with him, he would not respond or acknowledge that I was speaking to him.

Yet, another difficult student of mine came to class every day, participated in the study, was more than courteous, but would never turn in an assignment. She would tell me every day, do not take it personally, Mr. D., I just don't see the lifetime value in writing a paper about someone that I will never meet. This was a very difficult situation because she could be at the top of her class, but the difficulty in getting her to complete and turn in an assignment left me at a loss.

Difficult students may be challenging for other reasons than those associated with the discipline. I have experienced students that were difficult to understand, and they spoke perfect English, difficult to relate to because they prided themselves on not relating to adults. In my journey, the difficult student is the most "difficult" (for the lack of a better word) to work with. Why? I will ask you once again, what does difficult mean to you?

When I present at conferences and ask educators to define "difficult students," they all struggle. The funny thing is the term difficult student is often the most overused term associated with students with disciplinary problems. We use the term difficult almost as a default term as a catch-all for students that we cannot properly label or identify. This is a grave injustice on our behalf and shows just how mentally lazy we can become. We must properly identify why a student has been labeled or identified as difficult. Educators, I use the term "labeled" with a grain of salt; I am totally against labels of any sort. In Texas, we like to use the term "sub-population" to identify any group of non-white students. I challenge every colleague that has ever used that terminology. My argument is simply this, "we have student populations, not sub-populations. When we define a group as a sub, we are telling everyone that all other groups are more important than that particular group". So, please read the term labeled just as a synonym to identify and nothing else.

Educators working with difficult students must be effective teachers who discipline with encouragement and kind words much more often than rebukes or reprimands. The goal is to help students feel good about themselves and their behavior in the classroom.

Inevitably, though, misbehavior happens. When it does, keep the collected wisdom of experienced teachers in mind: Let's face it; if it were easy to work with difficult students, the word difficult would not be associated with them.

Proposed Strategies

1. Take a deep breath and try to remain calm. It is natural for frustration, resentment, and anger to overcome you. But when we are, we become less rational, and our agitation only adds fuel to an already hot situation. *Davis Model step 2, refrain from judgment.*

2. Try to set a positive tone and model an appropriate response, even if it means you must take a few moments to compose yourself. Acknowledge that you need time to think, time to respond. "This is upsetting me, too, but I need a few minutes to think before we talk about it." This

action demonstrates you are taking this very seriously, so much so that you had to take a moment before taking any action. *Davis Model step 4 be honest with your students.*

3. Make sure that the students understand that it is their misbehavior you dislike, not them. "I like you, Marcus. Right now, your behavior is unacceptable." We must avoid saying things like, "Marcus, this is one of the things that I dislike about you." Do not make it a personal attack.

4. Give the difficult student a chance to respond positively by explaining what they are doing wrong and what they can do to correct it. Validate the student as part of the process. *Davis Model step 4 & 5 be honest with our students and keep it simple and make deposits.*

5. Never resort to blaming or ridicule. *Davis Model step 2, refrain from judgment.*

6. Avoid win-lose conflicts. Emphasize problem-solving instead of punishment. *Davis Model step 5 keep it simple and make deposits.*

7. Try to remain courteous in the face of hostility or anger. Showing students that you care about them and their problems will help you earn their respect and establish rapport.

8. Be an attentive listener. Encourage students to talk out feelings and concerns and help them clarify their comments by restating them.

9. Model the behavior you expect from your students. Are you as considerate of your students' feelings as you want them to be of others? Are you as organized and on-task as you tell them to be? Are your classroom expectations clear and easy for students to follow?

10. Specifically, describe misbehavior and help students understand the consequences of misbehavior. Very young children may even need your explanations modeled or acted out.

11. Be aware of cultural differences. For example, some would view a student who stares at the floor while you speak to them as defiant and, in some cultures, as being respectful.

12. Discourage cliques and any other antisocial behavior. Offer cooperative activities to encourage group identity.

13. Teach students personal and social skills — communicating, listening, helping, and sharing, for example.

14. Teach students academic survival skills, such as paying attention, following directions, asking for help when they really need it, and volunteering to answer.

15. Avoid labeling students as "good" or "bad." Instead, describe their behavior as "positive," "acceptable," "disruptive," or "unacceptable."

16. Focus on recognizing and rewarding acceptable behavior more than punishing misbehavior.

17. Ignore or minimize minor problems instead of disrupting the class. A glance, a directed question, or your proximity may be enough to stop misbehavior.

18. Where reprimands are necessary, state them quickly and without disrupting the class.

19. When it is necessary to speak to a student about his or her behavior, try to speak in private; this is especially true of adolescents who must "perform" for their peers. Public reprimands or lectures often trigger exaggerated, face-saving performances.

Practice Scenario's

The following scenarios are about several difficult students. Read each scenario carefully, and in the space provided after each scenario, write down how you would utilize B.R.A.C.E. to support the student. Please feel free to refer to the Davis Relationship Model for Educators to help you develop your plan.

Difficult Student Maribel

Maribel is a fourth-grade student who has difficult times in social settings. She isolates himself in all settings; she has a very hard time in the classroom. Maribel would often yell out at any given moment. She would get up and roam around the classroom without permission. She would make odd noises constantly during class, and she would blurt out profanity at any given time.

Maribel was on a behavioral intervention plan and was very difficult to deal with.

Difficult Student:

Name: _____ School/Classroom: _____

City: _____ State: _____

How would you use Belief, Relationships, Attitude, Culture & Environment to support this student, and which B.R.A.C.E. elements would be most beneficial to this student?

_____

_____

_____

_____

_____

_____

_____

_____

_____

Difficult Student Sandra

Sandra was a senior in high school and lacked the motivation to work or achieve anything. Sandra was sitting in class day after day, looking at her assignments and spending most of her time applying makeup and combing her hair. Throughout her high school career, Sandra had been worked with individually often for the past three years. Some teachers had allowed Sandra to take her test using her notes or the teacher's notes. Other teachers allowed Sandra to complete her assignments on the tablet that would read the text to her. Both strategies only worked for a concise time. Sandra would abuse her privileges to use the tablet by visiting sites there were off-limits. Now in her senior year, Sandra is in jeopardy of graduating.

Difficult Student:

Name: _____ School/Classroom: _____

City: _____ State: _____

How would you use Belief, Relationships, Attitude, Culture & Environment to support this student, and which B.R.A.C.E. elements would be most beneficial to this student?

_____

_____

_____

_____

_____

_____

_____

_____

_____

Difficult Student Jesus

Jesus is a junior in high school in the state of Colorado. Jesus's teachers believe that he chooses to avoid doing what he should be doing, such as attending class and doing his work. Jesus loves to give excuses for why he is making the wrong choices. He places the blame on his friends, family life, and on occasion, family emergencies. When an adult tries to talk with Jesus about his actions, he pretends that he doesn't care, and it doesn't really matter to him. Jesus also likes to play the card that teachers do not like him. When asked to explain why he believes teachers do not like him, Jesus states, "I'm not going to tell you because you're not going to believe me anyway." Jesus is becoming very difficult to deal with because of his lack of accepting responsibility and his willingness to blame other people.

Difficult Student:

Name: _____ School/Classroom: _____

City: _____ State: _____

How would you use Belief, Relationships, Attitude, Culture & Environment to support this student, and which B.R.A.C.E. elements would be most beneficial to this student?

_____

_____

_____

_____

_____

_____

_____

_____

_____

Difficult Student:

Name: _____ School/Classroom: _____

City: _____ State: _____

How would you use Belief, Relationships, Attitude, Culture & Environment to support this student, and which elements of B.R.A.C.E. would be most beneficial to this student?

_____

_____

_____

_____

_____

_____

_____

_____

_____

Difficult Student:

Name: _____ School/Classroom: _____

City: _____ State: _____

How would you use Belief, Relationships, Attitude, Culture & Environment to support this student, and which B.R.A.C.E. elements would be most beneficial to this student?

_____

_____

_____

_____

_____

_____

_____

_____

_____

Disrespectful Students

━━━━━━━━━━━━━ ⌁⟨℘⟩⌁ ━━━━━━━━━━━━━

Disrespectful students present teachers with a real challenge. To be more precise, it is their behavior that is disrespectful. Our disrespectful students appear to come to school with one objective, "the world doesn't care about me – so I don't care about the world." These students' disrespectful levels know no bounds every day; their level of disrespect appears to escalate. It is as if they went home and took an online course in infinite ways to antagonize or disrespect others.

As educators, we often find ourselves wishing the school district offered these students the opportunity to take a Dale Carnegie course. Sorry for your young educators out there – Dale Carnegie was a famous author and lecturer who offered self-improvement and interpersonal skill development courses.

Students who behave disrespectfully tend to treat staff very discourteously. They roll their eyes, dismiss requests and instructions by 'talking back directly or indirectly,' and often act with utter disdain. When they are not sneering, they often ignore the teacher and generally act in a 'superior' manner, as if everything is 'beneath' them. Disrespectful students are experts at using this tactic. Let us face it; educators, our disrespectful students, make it truly hard not to take it personally. They often try to personalize their attacks to make the impact greater. Remember, their goal is to disrespect you or something that you are trying to teach. Therefore, it is crucial not to take our disrespectful students' actions personally. These small actions will take away the power that they perceive to have in our classrooms.

I know that a few teachers, educators, and administrators have gone home and just could not let whatever their disrespectful student had done go. Trust me when I say, "I get it." *I remember an occasion when one of my assistant principals and I were doing outside lunch duty. We were a closed campus and did not allow students to leave campus for lunch or to have their friends to bring them lunch onto the campus. On this day, my assistant got my attention and said, "look at who's trying to bring food onto campus." It was one of the rudest, most disrespectful students I have ever had in my education years. This student had once told her mother to shut the ** up. Fill in the asterixis. She had also shoved her dad out of her way. Back to this situation, we approached the student just as she exited her car. Excuse me, Miss Walters (not her real name), would you please show me your campus sign out pass that allows you to leave campus? The student ignored us and continued to get her lunch out of the car. I am sorry, you may not have heard me. Would you please show me your past, and this is a closed campus? You are not allowed to leave for lunch and bring food back onto campus. The student's comment to us was, "I don't have time to trip with you old **." My assistant principal then informed the student that you have two choices, (1) you can come with me to the office and call your parents and let them know that*

147

you left campus without permission. I will then explain to them our next step. (2) You can continue down the road you are currently on and have the school resource officer (SRO) involved. Either way, I will be calling your parents. The student turned to my assistant principal and, without notice, threw her 44-ounce drink in his face. Without hesitation, my assistant principal said, "now that was refreshing." I called the SRO on the radio to come over. The SRO detained the student until the parents arrived, and we let the parents know that she would be suspended, the SRO gave her a citation for assault, and we revoked her privilege to drive on campus for the remainder of the year. The parents offered to pay for my assistant principal's dry cleaning, but he declined and said that this was part of the job. That day he took this situation home with him, literally!

As with all behavior, there are likely to be some strong motives behind the actions displayed.

Acting disrespectful is often a way of disguising frustration and unhappiness; students like this may see behaving disrespectfully as a means of hurting other people, an act of revenge for times when they were hurt, perhaps by adults or by fellow students. Deep down, when students behave like this, they are often feeling quite fragile, and lashing out is a way of covering up this fragility.

This is the best time to get to the root of these behaviors. One conference I attended had a psychologist who was presenting on adult trauma. At this event, the psychologist made a statement during his presentation that has remained with me to this day. He said, "I am one of the most successful psychologists in the US when it comes to dealing with adult behavior because I don't treat the adult – I treat the child within the adult first, and then I treat the adult."

Now is the best time to treat whatever deep-seated thoughts or past issues our disrespectful student may have experienced.

Proposed Strategies

1. **Make it clear to the student that they have a choice** - if they continue to behave disrespectfully, there will be consequences - make them accept responsibility for their choice.

2. **Stay calm** - if we retaliate by being disrespectful back to the student, we're really letting them off the hook - we're conforming to the student that they're right to be disrespectful because of the adult world, the world of authority, is hostile towards them.

3. **If possible**, get the student alone, away from the 'audience' of the other students: if things develop into a public confrontation, the student may feel cornered, and this may provoke an even worse reaction, as the student attempts to save face - if it's at all possible, ask the student to go with you to another room where you can talk in private;

4. **Stay calm and listen first**: say to the student you don't appreciate being spoken to disrespectfully, but you can see the student must be upset about something, and you want to give the student a chance to explain why they've behaved in that way: it's important to let the student try to explain, and you need to listen first, try to understand before you try to make yourself understood;

5. **Staying calm maintains your credibility** with the whole class, not just the student in question: the class will respond better to someone who keeps their professional cool, and it takes away any excuse they may have for being hostile towards you - you've done nothing wrong, and you're trying to help the disrespectful student;

6. **Avoid making sarcastic comments** or trying to ridicule students with put-downs - this may well backfire on you because you'll end up alienating other students who see you being disrespectful and therefore feel you're giving them the green light to be disrespectful back to you

2-Things to Avoid

First, do not take it personally - you may well just be the unfortunate adult who happens

to be easily accessible to the student.

Secondly, you will not be able to get a student to stop being disrespectful by using force - it simply does not work and may well inflame the situation and make matters worse.

"No child
Ever became "good."
By being told
That she or he was "bad."

Maddy Malhotra

151

Additional Thoughts

Like many aspects of working with disrespectful behavior, it is easier said than done to remain calm and professional. We feel under attack ourselves but having a clear plan of strategies that you have rehearsed well mentally, gives a decent chance of managing the situation effectively.

You will need to follow up with the student later: you may need to refer the student to a counselor who may refer the student and parent to outside counseling. The point is to ensure that every adult with a contact within our setting is consistent in working with them. Make sure you let the student see that this is a natural stage of the process that's designed to help the student; it's not an opportunity to seek revenge and must be handled with the same professional calm and presence as when working with the initial incident.

> *"Where there is anger, there is always pain underneath"*
> *Eckhart Tolle*

Practice Scenario's

The following scenarios are about several disrespectful students. Read each scenario carefully, and in the space provided after each scenario, write down how you would utilize B.R.A.C.E. to support the student. Please feel free to refer to the Davis Relationship Model for Educators to help you develop your plan.

Disrespectful Student: Jacory

I was teaching at a junior/senior high school just outside of Tampa, Florida. It was a private school, and I was just promoted to Assistant Director but still had some teaching duties. A student that I had for a year already got very angry one day. His name is Jacory.

He was in my English class, and he failed a test. He became very disrespectful and demanded to know why he must learn English. He told me that he already knows how to speak English and wanted to learn Ebonics instead. He told me that I was pushing my culture and beliefs to him by making him take a class about 'the white man's language.' He stormed out of my classroom, and we gave him some time to calm down.

Later that day for lunch, I went and sat with him. We had a McDonalds across the street, so I had our teacher's aide run over there for me and grabbed lunch for Jacory and I. By this time, he had calmed down, so we got a chance to talk. Jacory was adopted at birth to a black father and a white mother. Sadly, he knew nothing about his biological parents, and this bothered him. His adopted fathers' side of the family had bullied him and told him that being raised by a white mother made him 'less' than a black man. He never shared this with his parents and let it fester inside him until he exploded in my classroom that day. He went on to tell me how he was longing to know more about his culture, background, and heritage and requested the Ebonics lesson as a way of asking for help.

We talked through lunch about better ways of expressing things that bother him and sharing his feelings and experiences with his father's family with his parents.

Jacory went on to graduate second in his class and has just finished a degree in radio production. I believe that all aspects of B.R.A.C.E helped in this situation. He saw that I wanted to build that relationship with him and gave him a comforting environment to open up and share with me.

Disrespectful Student:

Name: _____ School/Classroom: _____

City: _____ State: _____

How would you use Belief, Relationships, Attitude, Culture & Environment to support this student, and which B.R.A.C.E. elements would be most beneficial to this student?

_____

_____

_____

_____

_____

_____

_____

_____

_____

Disrespectful Student Sara

Sarah is a seventh-grade student in Louisiana. Sarah is a student that acts as if the world revolves around her. Sarah will purposely engage a student or teacher to get them off task. Sarah refuses to do what is asked by adults; Sara is the most disrespectful in these moments. Sarah will pretend not to hear the teacher or engage with another student saying, "I know that they're not speaking to me." Sarah's action is high when she speaks with an adult and does not respond that she would like. In these situations, Sarah responds by cursing, walking out of class, or merely putting on a dramatic display of emotions. When a teacher or administrator addresses Sarah's actions, Sarah often replies, "I know that you really don't care about me, so why should I really care about you and your class."

Disrespectful Student:

Name: _____ School/Classroom: _____

City: _____ State: _____

How would you use Belief, Relationships, Attitude, Culture & Environment to support this student, and which B.R.A.C.E. elements would be most beneficial to this student?

_____

_____

_____

_____

_____

_____

_____

_____

_____

Disrespectful Student:

Name: _____ School/Classroom: _____

City: _____ State: _____

How would you use Belief, Relationships, Attitude, Culture & Environment to support this student, and which B.R.A.C.E. elements would be most beneficial to this student?

_____

_____

_____

_____

_____

_____

_____

_____

Disrespectful Student:

Name: _____ School/Classroom: _____

City: _____ State: _____

How would you use Belief, Relationships, Attitude, Culture & Environment to support this student, and which B.R.A.C.E. elements would be most beneficial to this student?

_____

_____

_____

_____

_____

_____

_____

_____

_____

"Instead of viewing your most difficult student as a burden, Think of them as an opportunity to do your best work."

David Geurin

Disruptive Students

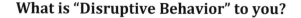

What is "Disruptive Behavior" to you?

Disruptive behavior is defined as repeated, continuous, and/or multiple student behaviors that hinder instructors' ability to teach and learn. This seems simple enough. Our disruptive students do not need to be provoked nor acknowledged; their purpose is to take the lead. Our disruptive students see the world through the eyes of a circus "Ringmaster" and are on center stage. Below is a list of common and extreme types of disruptive behavior. Educators, the below list is not a menu for us to pick from and compare with our building colleagues for war stories. Nor is it the call items for disruptive student bingo. In speaking with hundreds of classroom educators, building administrators, and central office administrators, these behaviors frequently appeared. Please understand that this list is not inclusive of every disruptive behavior that I have experienced. However, it is a list comprised of documented discipline issues that occur most often within our schools.

Common Types of Disruptive Behavior:

- Eating in class: This is easily remedied by having consistent classroom expectations.

- Monopolizing classroom discussions.
- Failing to respect the rights of other students to express their viewpoints.
- Carrying on distracting side conversations.
- Constant questions or interruptions which interfere with the instructor's presentation.
- Overt inattentiveness (e.g., sleeping, reading the paper, using laptops for non-class-related activities).
- Creating excessive noise with papers, book bags, etc.
- Entering class late or leaving early
- Use of cell phones in the classroom
- Inordinate or inappropriate demands for time and attention
- Poor personal hygiene (e.g., noticeably offensive body door)

Extreme Disruptions

- Use of profanity or pejorative language: I will never condone this type of behavior. If a student is constantly exhibiting profane or pejorative language in class or towards others, we must investigate the determining factors. This type of behavior is the proverbial "slip of the tongue."
- Intoxication: No Tolerance
- Verbal abuse (e.g., taunting, badgering, intimidation):
- Harassment (e.g., use of "fighting words," stalking)
- Threats to harm oneself or others

- Physical violence (e.g., shoving, grabbing, assault, use of weapons)

Proposed Strategies:

- Start making positive 'deposits' right away at the beginning of the semester. Show your enthusiasm for the subject and let them see that you are 100 percent committed to ensuring that each class will be a great experience for them. I have my teachers do this on the first day of class. If you have several deposits in your account, there will still be plenty of "respect funds" left in the account when you need them. *Davis Model step 5 keep it simple and make deposits.*

  For example, you may need to use some of your funds when getting firm with them, giving constructive criticism, or handing back lower than expected grades. If you have earned their respect and have made many deposits, you will find that they will not want to disappoint you and will try harder.

  However, if you start the first class with negative comments or actions, there is nothing in your 'account' to draw from later, and you will most likely be in the 'negatives' all semester. By the way, do not be pompous and say to them, "look to the left, look to the right... one of you will not make it." Because of the disruptive student, the one that will not make it is "you"!

- Remember the 3 R's: Rewards (Hand out free 'stuff,' positive feedback), Respect (do not ever talk 'down' to them), and Recognition (positive comments, certificates of recognition, helping with networking opportunities). *Davis Model steps #5, #2 and #3, keep it simple and make deposits, refrain from judgment, and persistent communication.*

- Day one, look in the back row and back corners of the classroom to see who is sitting there. Nothing has really changed since high school; many of the 'unmotivated' students are usually sitting there. After all, isn't it the best place to sit to be 'off the radar' and not pay attention? Make sure to walk around the class when you teach and hover around those areas before you see 'chatter' (verbal or texting) going on.

- If students are talking, simply walk over to where they are sitting and lecture there for a while. If you want, give them your best 'I'm not impressed' glance.

- Ask the students who are talking if they have a question. Stop midway through your sentence if you must. The answer will most likely be "No." The awkwardness of the situation usually stops the conversation.

- Give students a small 'brain break' after 10-15 minutes (frequent small group purposeful talks from the Fundamental 5). This break is meant only to be for 3-minutes and is not meant for students to leave the class. It will allow just enough time to quickly talk about the sports game or party last night or text their friends.

- If a student's behavior is becoming an ongoing issue, talk to them in the hall during break hours and not in front of their peers. Tell them that the chatter (verbal or text) distracts you from doing your job of teaching him/her and the rest of the class. The point is, do not let it slide; talk to them sooner than later. Depending on the classroom expectations, an email to the students, AP may need to be written, and the student may need to meet with him/her.

- Talk to your students on their breaks, after class, or when you see them in the hall about non-subject topics (music, sports). Get to know them on a more personal level and find out about their interests. You can even send them an article of interest or link to a video that they would like outside class time. This will eliminate a 'you vs. them' scenario in class. Non-clamantly read a quick list of their classroom management (top 10 list?) during the first class; it will set the tone and address potential future issues right away.

Practice Scenario's

The following scenarios are about several disruptive students. Read each scenario carefully, and in the space provided after each scenario, write down how you would utilize B.R.A.C.E. to support the student. Please feel free to refer to the Davis Relationship Model for Educators to help you develop your plan.

Disruptive Student: Mike

Mike is an eighth-grade student at a local middle school in Texas. It is an everyday occurrence for Mike to act out in class. He walks from the classroom disrupting class in the following manner: he yells out at other students; when the teacher asks him to lower his voice, he yells louder and starts arguments with other students. Mike often tries to provoke students verbally as well as physical altercations. When teachers or administrators address Mike and his behavior, he starts to cry, and when consequences are being discussed, he cries erratically. While being addressed by adults', Mike will sit, refusing to stand, make eye contact, and refusing to acknowledge the adult. When teachers or administrators inform Mike that they will be contacting a parent, he becomes very belligerent, insisting that they do not contact his father. There have been multiple occasions where an administrator and the school resource officer had to remove Mike from the classroom.

Disruptive Student:

Name: _____ School/Classroom: _____

City: _____ State: _____

How would you use Belief, Relationships, Attitude, Culture & Environment to support this student, and which elements of B.R.A.C.E. would be most beneficial to this student?

_____

_____

_____

_____

_____

_____

_____

_____

_____

Disruptive Student Michelle

Michelle is a junior student at a local high school; she is currently talking out in class when not working. Michelle has a comment to make on nearly every action in the classroom that involves other students. Michelle needs the attention and approval from her peers. When a teacher or administrator approaches Michelle about her activities, she becomes very defensive. During passing periods, class time, and all school transition times, Michelle is the loudest student. It would be easy to assume that Michelle is a leader; however, upon closer investigation, most students follow her to prevent being bullied. Michelle's actions and behavior are so disruptive that she has a file in the administrative office with more than 50 entries from the first semester alone.

Disruptive Student:

Name: _____ School/Classroom: _____

City: _____ State: _____

How would you use Belief, Relationships, Attitude, Culture & Environment to support this student, and which B.R.A.C.E. elements would be most beneficial to this student?

_____

_____

_____

_____

_____

_____

_____

_____

Disruptive Student Brandon

Brandon is a fourth-grade student in California, is a child of a military family. Because of Brandon's family military background, he has moved around quite a bit. In speaking with his father, Brandon has attended four elementary schools in the past six years. Brandon's longest amount of time has ever attended any one school in grades pre-K, kindergarten, and midway through his first-grade school year. The constant moving from one geographical region to another and school to school has made it difficult for Brandon to make friends. In reviewing Brenda's discipline records from each of his previous campuses, they all read the same. Here's an example; "Brandon is a brilliant child; however, he chooses to use his intelligence to disrupt the learning environment by being the class clown. It is not uncommon for Brandon to yell out, I cannot do this assignment because I don't have a pencil. Whenever the teacher walks by, Brandon will make audible noises with his mouth. On several occasions, Brandon has engaged his class in fictional stories about him, his dog, and his best friend, Sam. The truth is Brandon does not have a dog, and his friends Sam is make-believe. Brandon is currently being redirected by the teacher for his behavior in class".

Disruptive Student:

Name: _____ School/Classroom: _____

City: _____ State: _____

How would you use Belief, Relationships, Attitude, Culture & Environment to support this student, and which B.R.A.C.E. elements would be most beneficial to this student?

_____

_____

_____

_____

_____

_____

_____

_____

Disruptive Student:

Name: _____ School/Classroom: _____

City: _____ State: _____

How would you use Belief, Relationships, Attitude, Culture & Environment to support this student, and which B.R.A.C.E. elements would be most beneficial to this student?

_____

_____

_____

_____

_____

_____

_____

_____

_____

Disruptive Student:

Name: _____ School/Classroom: _____

City: _____ State: _____

How would you use Belief, Relationships, Attitude, Culture & Environment to support this student, and which B.R.A.C.E. elements would be most beneficial to this student?

_____

_____

_____

_____

_____

_____

_____

_____

_____

Content, Culture & Conversations

We have looked at quite a bit of information in this book thus far. I expect that the scenarios, positive affirmations, and quotes are included along our journey to support our learning. Beliefs, Relationship, Attitude, Culture, and Environment (B.R.A.C.E.) are essential in our school districts, schools, classrooms, and, most importantly, our students' success. We may not be able to reach and connect with 100 percent of our students, but as educators, it is our job – no, it is our responsibility to try and reach and connect with them. I would like to see school districts, schools, administrators, and teachers make the same commitment to B.R.A.C.E. that we do to increase our academic data.

Remember that comment earlier about the "two biggest district and campus mistakes"?

1. Focusing on the "data" before validating the "culture."
2. Building solutions around their "data" without studying their existing "culture".

The following are a few campus examples of placing content before culture and the results that we can expect. Remember, Google can teach content, but it cannot build a culture. When the "search engine" boom happened, I was in college! Many of you may not remember some of the following search engines; Ask Jeeves, Momma, Dogpile, Lycos, Alta Vista, Excite, and Web Crawler. These search engines existed long before Google, and each was filled with content, yet they are no longer around. Many of our former colleagues fall into this same category – they knew the content, they were recognized as extremely smart, but they are no longer around. Our children need adults and educators who can fill their lives with more than content.

Mathematics Class

It has always amazed me how our math teachers will lecture on finding "X." For example, if the equation we need to find "X" in the equation, $2X + 18 = 0$". You must first isolate $2X$ by subtracting both sides.

The next step would be to divide both sides by -2. The final step would calculate the solution by dividing 18 by -2, "X" would equal a -9. Every math teacher understands that to find "X," they must first isolate. This is one lesson that most students, regardless of their grade point average, understand clearly. However, many math teachers fail to understand the value of isolating our 4-D students from their behavior to work with our students and help them. We must understand our students and their individual needs.

Science Class

I have walked into many science labs and observed labs on how speaking to plants will help stimulate the plant's growth and how speaking positively to the same plant will cause even more growth. Yet, every year many science teachers miss out on the lab in their classrooms each day—speaking positively to our 4-D students that walk into their classrooms and helping them grow. Remember, people before plants, even in the dictionary.

History Class

What about the history teacher that lectures passionately about the impact of learning from our past so that we will not be destined to have history repeat itself? Our history teachers plan lessons on some of the most successful leadership strategies in history. They walk students through a step by step detailed illustration of why these leadership strategies were destined to be successful. Some teachers often never see the power of leadership strategies and their connections to our 4-D students. These very same teachers find it hard to understand why their discipline issues with our 4-D students continue to repeat year after year.

English Class

Okay, I do not forget about our English teacher because it looks like I am pointing out all our core subject areas and left them out. English teachers will make it a point that every student understands the five points of writing.

1. Organization (must have a thesis statement in the introduction and the remainder of the essay must support the thesis statement).

2. Progression of the story (watch out for repetition of words and ideas; the story must move forward).

3. Development of Ideas with a personal experience and specific examples.

4. Use of language (word choice) makes the reader see and feel what you are trying to say.

5. Conventions (sentence structure, punctuation, and spelling).

With a focus on writing strategies such as these, we expect all students to write an effective essay or composition. One would think that when educators work together to break down and plot out simple but effective writing strategies to support student learning, surely, they could do the same to support our 4-D students. There are still teachers out there who do not see the benefits of putting in the same amount of work they used to develop writing strategies to develop strategies to work with our 4-D students. These teachers and educators have a belief that their job is to teach content over teaching students.

The point is this, as we spend a great deal of time and money focusing on ways to deliver and increase data understanding. We spend almost no time devising strategies to support our 4-D students' and classroom success related to the data.

History has a list of failed organizations because they focused on changing or impacting their data or bottom line and ignored their culture. Thousands of organizations fall prey to this elementary mistake every year. It is an easy mistake to make. Human nature is to see a problem and solve said problem. If sales are down in kitchen appliances, seek ways to increase sales in the kitchen appliance department. The answer is no; we would need to look at all the contributing cultural factors first. What brands do we carry? Are we cost-competitive, are consumers aware of our location, and our sales associates' motivations? Do we have sales associate paid by the hour and make the same weekly salary no matter how many appliances we sell, or are our sales associates hourly plus commission and thus can earn more money based on the number of appliances sold. Hourly employees have zero motivation to increase appliance sales. Their paycheck will remain the same despite the lack of success of the department. Commissioned based employees understand that their income is based on the success of their sales. Thus, the better the department makes, the more money they will make. **B.R.A.C.E.**

B.R.A.C.E. is equally important to our academic achievements as well. We expect to make every major change through our beliefs, relationships, attitudes, culture, and environment. In Fourteen years in corporate America and my 20 plus years in education, I firmly believe in "people, not programs." People can make connections and deepen trust.

If you have been in education long enough, you have worked in or heard about a district that rolled out a very expensive district-wide program that was intended to change life as we know it. These districts spend a lot of money sending every employee in the district to train, and they pay an additional monetary amount to have an in-house consultant to be used as the district expert. Here is an example from a district that I am aware of. The state had designated the district as being out of compliance for disproportionately disciplining minority students. In response to the state's designation, the district adopted a program designed to build connections between minority students and teachers. The program's cost, the training, and the district consultant equivalently hired several new teachers. Great idea, right? In theory, yes; however, the district leadership team did not bother to validate their current culture. Had the district leadership team taken the time to monitor and survey the district educators, they would have realized one very important concern. Most teachers, administrators, and paraprofessionals were highly adult-centered, and very student punitive. Because the district's educators' culture was that the students were the issue, not disciplining students, the district's new initiative was not well received. About five and a half months into the school year, the district abandons the program.

The program that the district had adopted was a research-based best practice and proven program. However, when adults fail to see their need for any program, the program's success is destined to fail. People before programs, we must know what the fabric of our district, campus, and classroom culture is telling us.

When working with our 4-D students, our teachers must base their success on how successful they are. Teachers and administrators must move past our current focus on teaching and move towards a true focus on learning. One of my most liked sayings is, "it's not what teachers cover; it's what students discover." Showing our 4-D students and all our students that we as educators truly care will open a whole world of discovery. As educators, let us stop placing teaching before learning and content over culture and climate. Data will always tell us where we are as a campus and district. Culture will continue to be the narrative of how we got there as a campus and district.

Keep It in The B.A.G.
Behavior-Attendance-Grades

Before we go, I want to touch on an area that will happen on our campus, no matter how hard we try to prevent it. We will have student/parent/teacher conferences and/or a student/parent/ teacher/ administrator conference. When these meetings occur, if we have not implemented B.R.A.C.E. as educators, it will come up in these meetings. Our parents are going to take most of these meetings personally, not on purpose. But let's put ourselves in their position, they are more than likely missing work, and the meetings are typically not about their child's success. Yes, you are correct; some of our meetings are about student success.

What I want to discuss right now is this, parents are going to come to the school—knowing that we firmly believe that only the 4-D student's parents schedule parent conferences and are the parents most likely to be called to the school. This is not true by any means. Parents come to our campuses for several reasons. When the parents of our 4-D students show up, we know that it's not going to be a celebration of student success most of the time. The following is something that I have shared with teachers, administrators, and central office administrator for the past twenty-plus years. This straightforward approach to parent meetings has saved many a relationship with my teachers and parents.

First, let's start with this in mind. It does not matter what the reason for the meeting; please let the parent speak first. Know that what we have to say is as important to the meeting as what the parent must talk about. "Not true"! Many times, when we as educators speak first in these meetings, we often fuel the meeting to go in a whole new direction. What I am about to suggest will work if you have prior notice to the parent coming to campus or a parent drive by.

Here is my big share, whenever we meet with parents, never make it, or take it personally. As an educator, our focus in a parent meeting should always and only keep the meeting in the "bag." The "bag" is the student's behavior, attendance and/or grades. This is not the time to discuss all the B.R.A.C.E. components that you have employed in your classroom. Just keep the discussion topics on the "bag" this will help steer the conference conversation away from personal attacks by you, the teacher, and the parent.

After the parent has had an opportunity to speak what is on their mind, it is now is our time to speak. "Mr. and Mrs. Johnson, I am so happy to meet you. You can apologize here if it is an unfortunate situation. "I am sorry that our first meeting is under these circumstances, but we are all here to help your student." If it is not an unfortunate situation, thank and acknowledge the parent for coming to the school.

"The parent/teacher conference is not the time to get even with the student who has wreaked havoc in your classroom all year long. It's the time to start making repairs to your student-parent relationship." Larry D. Davis

Our next discussion point will be something like this; "I would like to talk about ways that I can work with you to help (say the student's name) remain successful or become more successful. Try your best to refrain from using the word fail in any format. How can we keep your student from failing? Currently, your student is failing; your student is failing because of their...? If the student is failing; simply say, "your student's success is in jeopardy; I want to discuss how we can support them and keep this from happening." Our words will linger and come back to haunt us if we do not choose our word carefully.

Now, it is time to discuss the student's behavior, attendance and/or grades. "Mr. and Mrs. Johnson, your student's success is in jeopardy at this time because of their behavior, attendance, or grades; these are the areas we need to support you with." Nothing personal about how you feel about the student, no personal attacks on the parents' parenting skills, or lack thereof. Keep it in the B.A.G., and I will almost guarantee you a meeting that will end quickly and positively.

If the students are in good standing behavior-wise, have good attendance, and their grades indicate that they are performing well. As educators, we are more than likely not meeting with their parents. When we focus on the things that show measures and demonstrate an ability to develop strategies to support students, parents tend to leave our campuses happy.

As educators, when we can commit to B.R.A.C.E. in our classrooms, our schools, and in the school districts, we are committing to changing lives, caring for our students, and ultimately changing the optics of how the world will see our schools.

> *"Children must have at least one person*
> *who believes in them?*
> *It could be you."*
>
> Marian Wright Edelman

The Spirit of an Educator

I once sat in these desks as a student,

Today, I stand before those very desks as a teacher.

How lucky am I? At work, each day

I get to help children learn and succeed, and keep them safe so
they will grow

I get to open minds that are unlike mine.

I teach children with different names and faces,

I see their beautiful minds, not their beautiful races.

I know I play an important part in inspiring them to take learning
to heart.

How grateful am I? I value this so much.

The dreams I support and the lives I touch.

Today I stand before young scholars, but tomorrows who knows
who they may become.

So, I take pride in educating these young scholars one by one.

I will continue to educate all children regardless of the struggles
and strife,

Because I realize that education is the cure to a common life.

by Larry D. Davis

"In the end, it will be impossible to know if we overreacted or did too much; but it will be quite apparent if we under reacted or did too little!" by Leadership Matters

"Education Needs A Champion" This is why we exist!

ABOUT THE AUTHOR

Larry Davis's "Why" is to "Champion an education system where every educator, teacher and school leaders will make our children a priority. Where every child will experience an educational system that will make their care, learning and unique individual talents our focus. Where champion educators, teachers and school leaders do more to increase our student's achievement and success, to do more to grow and support our teachers and to do more to realize the mission and vision of our school district. Why? Because "Education Needs a Champion!"

Larry D. Davis passion for education and learning is second only to his love of God and his children. Larry's experience is broad and extensive, which includes being a classroom teacher, assistant principal, house principal, high school principal, district coordinator for school improvement, district coordinator for college and career readiness/CTE/IB Programs, regional director and is currently the executive director of secondary education and talent development. Davis also spent 15 years in corporate America in various leadership positions.

Larry is an honored graduate of Eastern Hills High School, located in Fort Worth, Texas. Larry received his Associates Degree from Weatherford College in Weatherford, Texas, his bachelor's degree from the University of Texas at Arlington in Arlington, Texas. He earned his master's degree from Texas Woman's University located in Denton, Texas.

Larry believes that education has forgotten that children are our why and our reason for what we do each day. Somewhere between high stakes testing and increased accountability, education has become more about the adult, the districts, and the policy makers. Davis says that once we remove all the hidden agendas and politics from our education system, the children of this country will once again become our focus.

Education needs a champion; this is why we exist.